CHANGING OF THE GODS

CHANGING OF THE

gods

FEMINISM
AND THE END OF
TRADITIONAL
RELIGIONS

Naomi R. Goldenberg

Beacon Press   Boston

Copyright © 1979 by Naomi R. Goldenberg

Beacon Press books are published under the auspices
of the Unitarian Universalist Association

Published simultaneously in Canada by
Fitzhenry & Whiteside Ltd., Toronto

Printed in the United States of America

(hardcover) 9 8 7 6 5 4 3 2

Portions of this book have previously appeared
in *Signs: Journal of Women in Culture and
Society; International Journal of Women's
Studies; Anima; Psychocultural Review;* and
*Spring — An Annual of Archetypal Psychology
and Jungian Thought.*

Grateful acknowledgment is made to the following:
Susan Stern for permission to quote her work
"Invocation to the Goddess" and Miriam Simos
(Starhawk) for permission to quote her two
works "Invocations to the Guardians of the
Watchtowers" and "Queen of the Night."

Library of Congress Cataloging in Publication Data
Goldenberg, Naomi R
    Feminism and the end of traditional religions.
    Bibliography: p.
    Includes index.
    1. Women and religion.   2.   Religions (Proposed,
universal, etc.) 3. Psychology, Religious. 4.
Christianity — Controversial literature. 5. Judaism
— Controversial literature. 6. Feminism — Moral
and religious aspects. I. Title.
BL458.G64 1979   291.1'7834'12   78-19602
ISBN 0-8070-1110-X

FOR CAROL P. CHRIST

and for Herb, Evelyn and Sadie

With thanks to Margaret Farley, Naomi Scheman,
Rosemary Ruether, Peter Slater
and R. Paul Brady

CONTENTS

Chapter 1

THE END AND THE BEGINNING

WHAT WILL HAPPEN TO God?" I first asked myself this question in 1971. I was sitting in a circle of women in Westchester, New York. We were all "housewives" with families and homes to care for. Some of us worked outside the home as well. It was the first consciousness-raising group I had ever attended.

Each woman had agreed to address the question "What prevented me from doing something I wanted to do?" I spoke about my recent decision to leave graduate school before completing my degree. I had been studying classics. I told the group that if anything had prevented me from earning my doctorate it was the subject of classics itself. It seemed that most of what the present generation of classical scholars did was describe the work of the past generation of classical scholars. Nothing new was happening. Although I enjoyed university life and although I felt work as a scholar was my true vocation, I could not bear research that was done as if it were ritual — research that was undertaken for the sake of proving you could endure the tedium of citing obscure texts and checking the even more obscure references to those texts. If I ever went back to graduate school, I had promised myself it would be to study something new — something that mattered in the evolution of human culture.

Most of the other women also discussed their failure to

achieve particular career goals. Some had begun training to become lawyers, journalists or doctors and felt that either family conflicts or the discouragement of male teachers and colleagues had caused them to drop out. A few felt that they didn't have enough energy to pick up the same career aspirations again.

Several women, however, had more hope. They were beginning their training all over again — this time armed with political insight, which they felt would enable them to understand the sexism they were bound to encounter and to suffer through it to attain their objectives. They intended to "stay women," that is, preserve the values they had learned in their years as mothers and housewives and to bring those values to their work. Likewise, they intended to "stay feminists" and remain committed to the political ideals of equal dignity and opportunity for both sexes. These women were realists who fully expected to work hard their whole lives at careers in which their gender and their politics would prove to be handicaps.

I enjoyed listening to the determination in their voices. "Such women will change the world," I thought. I felt that when enough women like them entered traditional professions, the structure of those professions could not remain the same. Female values and female ways of life would eventually have to be accommodated by the male hierarchies and would transform the hierarchies themselves. I felt I was living at the beginning of a major social revolution and wanted to participate with any talent I might possess.

The most important story I heard that night was one of a woman who had wanted to be a minister. She had begun study at Drew University, but had dropped out after a year and a half of course work. "They didn't know how to act around me in seminary classes," she said. "The men all kept asking me why I wanted to be a minister and expected me to give up. I had to argue with them and justify myself every day. I finally left seminary." This woman had no intention of ever going back. "The clergy can't accept women in their ranks," she said.

" WHAT WILL HAPPEN TO GOD?"

"The clergy will have to accept women," I thought. The feminist revolution will not leave religion untouched. Eventually, all religious hierarchies would be peopled with women. I imagined women functioning as rabbis, priests and ministers. I pictured women wearing clerical garb and performing clerical duties and suddenly *I saw a problem.* How could women represent a male god?

Everything I knew about Judaism and Christianity involved accepting God as the ultimate in male authority figures. If enough women claimed to represent "His" authority — to embody "His" presence in synagogues and on pulpits — congregations would have to stop seeing God as male. God would begin to look like "His" female officials. "And what would these women priests, ministers and rabbis read to their communities?" I wondered. They could certainly not use the Bible. A society that accepted large numbers of women as religious leaders would be too different from the biblical world to find the book relevant, let alone look to it for inspiration.

"God is going to change," I thought. "We women are going to bring an end to God. As we take positions in government, in medicine, in law, in business, in the arts and, finally, in religion, we will be the end of Him. We will change the world so much that He won't fit in anymore."

I found this line of thought most satisfying. I had no great tie to God anyway. He never seemed to be relevant to me at all. Reflection on His cultural demise left me with no sense of loss. Yet there was a magnificence attached to the idea of watching Him go. I felt part of a movement that would challenge religions that had been in force for millennia. "What will happen to God in His last years?" I wondered. "And who or what will replace Him?" I knew these were important questions. Here was no issue of only scholarly interest. The end of God and the transformation of religion was of major significance to human life. I decided to spend some of my own life thinking about it. Two months after that consciousness-raising meeting in Westchester I returned to graduate school to study the end of God.

FEMINISTS ARE COOKING UP GÖTTERDÄMMERUNG

The feminist movement in Western culture is engaged in the slow execution of Christ and Yahweh. Yet very few of the women and men now working for sexual equality within Christianity and Judaism realize the extent of their heresy.

Within Christianity, devout Catholic and Protestant women are rewriting liturgies to refer to "sisters" as well as to "brothers," calling attention to the importance of women in the story of Christ and seeking ordination as ministers and priests in greater numbers than ever before. Within Judaism, loyal Jewish women are improvising ceremonies to celebrate the birth of daughters as well as sons, establishing the right of females to be included in the *minyan*,[1] and founding publications that challenge the inferior position of women in the Jewish religion.[2]

The Jewish and Christian women who are reforming their traditions do not see such reforms as challenging the basic nature of Christianity and Judaism. Instead, they understand themselves to be improving the practice of their religions by encouraging women to share the responsibilities of worship equally with men.

As a psychologist of religion, I do not agree that improving the position of women is a minor alteration in Judaeo-Christian doctrine. The reforms that Christian and Jewish women are proposing are major departures from tradition. When feminists succeed in changing the position of women in Christianity and Judaism, they will shake these religions at their roots. The nature of a religion lies in the nature of the symbols and images it exalts in ritual and doctrine. It is the psychic picture of Christ and Yahweh that inspires the loves, the hates and the behavior patterns of Christians and Jews. The psychology of the Jewish and Christian religions depends on the masculine image that these religions have of their God. Feminists change the major psychological impact of Judaism and Christianity when they recognize women as religious leaders and as images of divinity.

The Wisdom of Pope Paul

Conservative leaders of contemporary religious institutions understand that allowing women access to top positions of authority threatens the age-old composition of the institutions themselves.

In January 1977, Pope Paul VI issued a declaration affirming the Vatican's ban on allowing women to be ordained as Catholic priests. The document states that because Christ was a man and because he chose only male disciples, women can never serve as chief officials in the Catholic hierarchy.

Pope Paul used an impressive knowledge of how image and symbol operate in the human mind to build his case against female priests. "The priest," he explained, "is a sign . . . a sign that must be perceptible and which the faithful must be able to recognize with ease. The whole sacramental economy is in fact based upon natural signs, on symbols imprinted upon the human psychology. 'Sacramental signs,' says St. Thomas, 'represent what they signify by natural resemblance. . . .' When Christ's role in the Eucharist is to be expressed sacramentally, there would not be this 'natural resemblance' which must exist between

Christ and His minister if the role of Christ were not taken by a man. In such a case it would be difficult to see in the minister the image of Christ. For Christ himself was and remains a man."[3]

Pope Paul reasoned that because the priest must represent Christ, i.e., God, the priest must resemble God. If the priest looked very different from Christ, a follower would not feel an immediate connection between God and the priest who was supposed to embody *Him.* The Pope realized that people experience God through *His* representatives. If one were to change the sex of God's representatives, one would be changing the nature of God *Himself.* As the chief guardian of the Catholic faith, the Pope understood that he could not allow any serious tampering with the image of God.

Pope Paul went on to explain that men and women have different roles in Christianity. "Equality is in no way identity," he said, "for the Church is a differentiated body in which each individual has his or her role. The roles are distinct and must not be confused."[4] These roles, the Pope insisted, "do not favor the superiority of some vis-à-vis the others."[5]

This statement falls short of the intelligence informing most of the document. Feminists understand that if women are not sufficiently "in the image of God" to be priests, then they are certainly considered inferior to men. No amount of prose extolling the harmony of keeping men and women in "separate but equal" roles can change the fact that men are reserving the most important roles for themselves. To gain true equality in Christianity women must have access to the positions that religion holds to be highest and best.

Change Is Inevitable

At the present moment, no major Christian denomination has more than a few token women in top authority positions. However, this exclusion is short-lived. In a few more decades, sizable numbers of women ministers will graduate from Protestant seminaries and will take charge of parishes throughout the Western world. Liberal Catholics will eventually win their fight to have women ordained as priests. The recognition of large numbers of women as Christian spiritual leaders will advance the personal dignity and social privilege of females everywhere.

However, we must ask ourselves what will happen to Christianity when women do succeed in changing traditions so that they are treated as the equals of men. Will not this major departure from the Christian view of women radically alter the religion? Pope Paul knew it would. The Pope understood that representatives of Christianity mirror the image of God by calling to mind the male figure of Jesus Christ. If women play at being priests, they would play at being God; and Christianity, he insisted, can only afford to have men in that role.

Although Jewish leaders do not argue against female equality in the same terms as Pope Paul did, they must respect Jewish law and tradition. This is the essence of Judaism — to the same extent that the nature of Christ is the essence of Christianity. The role and image of females in Jewish law is very different from that of males. The law is supposed to make women — again the familiar phrase — separate but equal. Yet men perform the most important acts of religious duty and women are seen as people who prepare food and tend home and children so that men may be free to worship and study Torah. In orthodox synagogues, women sit apart from men so as not to distract them. In synagogues in which this physical separation is not enforced women are separated from men by the words of Talmud and Torah, which instruct females to be content with their subordinate roles in the Jewish community. The nature of the religion lies in interplay between a father-god and His sons. In such a religion, women will always be on the periphery. When Jewish women take a central place in their religion, they will no longer be practicing Judaism.

NEW GODS ARE COMING

Many scholars of religion disagree with the radical direction I have predicted. They say that Christianity and Judaism can survive the very basic changes that will have to be made when these religions adapt to nonsexist culture. These scholars insist that a religion is whatever its followers define it to be. Christianity and Judaism, therefore, are said to consist of whatever those who call themselves Christians and Jews practice as religion. Theoretically then, Christianity could exist without Christ and Judaism could exist without Yahweh's laws as long as Christians and Jews *thought* of these departures from tradition as being in basic harmony with their faiths. Texts could be altered, female imagery could be added to the concept of God, new rituals and doctrines could be invented without bringing about the end of the faiths. Scholars who believe this is possible point out that Western religions have survived many changes over the past centuries and can be expected to survive many more in years to come.

I wonder. Judaism and Christianity have never been challenged to the extent that they will be in the next decades. The images of Christ and Yahweh will be questioned because of the very basic quality of maleness. All of the roles that men and women have been taught to consider as God-given will be re-evaluated. Although it is certainly true that small groups of Christians and Jews have departed from tradition by conceiving of God in female terms and by experimenting with new roles for men and women,[6] such sects have been rather small-scale religious anomalies. The women's movement will bring about religious changes on a massive scale. These changes will not be restricted to small numbers of individuals practicing nonsexist religions within a sexist society. Society itself will be transformed to the point that it will no longer be a patriarchy. For if men are no longer supreme rulers on earth, how could one expect them to retain sovereignty in heaven?

There will of course be nothing to prevent people who practice new religions from calling themselves Christians or Jews. Undoubtedly, many followers of new faiths will still cling to old labels. But a merely semantic veneer of tradition ought not to hide the fact that very nontraditional faiths will be practiced. Those of us who fancy ourselves scholars of religion will perceive what is happening more clearly if we do not pretend that we are watching minor metamorphoses occurring within the Jewish and Christian traditions.

What will we be watching? What sort of religious forces are beginning in this era of death for the great male gods? Surely new gods will be born. Since "gods" always reflect the styles of behavior we see as possible, as our range of the possible expands so must our pantheon.

Up until very recently, the only kind of legitimate public authority most of us could imagine was that of an adult male. As long as this image held us, we could picture God only as an old man. Now a growing number of us are able to imagine authority in new guises. Feminism is pushing us into an age of experimentation with new personifications of authority. We can picture public power held by a woman or group of women, shared by both sexes or rotated between the sexes. These more fluid concepts of hierarchy are certain to affect our view of God. In order for systems of religions to prove inspiring in this new age such ideals of pluralism and experimentation will have to be reflected in religious doctrine and practice.

Chapter 2

NO FEMINIST CAN SAVE GOD

eVERY WOMAN working to improve her own position in society or that of women in general is bringing about the end of God. All feminists are making the world less and less like the one described in the Bible and are thus helping to lessen the influence of Christ and Yahweh on humanity.

Women engaged in the formal study of religion are more directly involved in the religious revolution that feminism is accomplishing. Some of these women are advocating the complete abandonment of Judaism and Christianity. Others are trying to save Judaism and Christianity by reform of the sexist practices in their traditions. Although I admire the energy of the reformers, I see them engaged in a hopeless effort. Analysis of their work reveals the futility of any attempt to defend patriarchal creeds.

The first feminist critic of biblical traditions understood that Judaism and Christianity had to be eliminated for the position of women to be significantly improved. In 1895 American suffragist Elizabeth Cady Stanton and her revising committee began work on *The Woman's Bible*. Stanton wanted people to realize how much the Bible degraded women. Many feminists of the day opposed Stanton's project because they thought such a controversial undertaking might harm their political cause. Susan B. Anthony gave a more "practical" reason. "No," she said in a letter to Stanton, "I don't want my name on that Bible committee — *You* fight that battle — and leave me to fight the secular — the political fellows. . . . I simply don't want the enemy to be diverted from my practical ballot fight — to that of scoring me for belief one way or the other about the Bible." A few years later, Anthony told Stanton that "the like of you ought to stop hitting poor old St. Paul — and give your heaviest raps on the head of every Nabob — man or woman who does injustice to a human being — for the 'crime' of color or sex!!"[1] Anthony's preference for secular issues was shared by many women in the movement.

However, although Stanton's bible was viewed as peripheral or even antithetical to the pragmatic efforts of nineteenth-century suffragists, the book had a thoroughly practical motive. Elizabeth Cady Stanton was tired of hearing the scriptures used to hold women back. "These familiar texts," she charged "are quoted by clergymen in their pulpits, by statesmen in the halls of legislation, by lawyers in the courts, and are echoed by the press of all civilized nations, and are accepted by woman herself as 'The Word of God.' So perverted is the religious element in her nature, that with faith and works she is the chief support of the church and clergy; the very powers that make her emancipation impossible. When, in the early part of the nineteenth century, women began to protest against their civil and political degradation, they were referred to the Bible for an answer. When they protested against their unequal position in the church, they were referred to the Bible for an answer."[2]

Stanton's quarrel with the Bible is basically legalistic. She objected to using the book as an authority to justify the unequal treatment of women in society. Several writers have remarked on how blind she seemed to be to the metaphoric and symbolic qualities of the scriptures. Aesthetics certainly was never Stanton's primary interest.

Almost every entry she signed in *The Woman's Bible* slips into invective against the customs and laws which the Bible supports. "The Mosaic code," she asserted, "is responsible for the religious customs of our own day and generation. Church property all over this broad land is exempt from taxation while the smallest house and lot of every poor widow is taxed at its full value."[3] This statement is typical of Stanton's style. Her major objective was to undermine biblical authority and she used almost any means to do this. She pointed out absurdities, underlined contradictions and suggested misinterpretations on the part of male scholars.

Stanton discussed each action or attitude of a biblical character much as a lawyer might do in trying to convince a jury of the good or bad features in a client's behavior. When she found a good character such as Deborah, she regretted the lack of publicity: "We never hear sermons pointing women to the heroic virtues of Deborah as worthy of their imitation."[4] When she found a bad character such as Abraham, she inveighed against him: "Abraham does not appear in a very attractive light, rising early in the morning and sending his child and its mother forth into the wilderness, with a breakfast of bread and water, to care for themselves. Why did he not provide them with a servant, an ass laden with provisions, and a tent to shelter them from the elements, or better still, some abiding resting place?"[5] Stanton's analysis of literary characters had to be literal because her opponents were using these characters as literalisms against her political cause. Biblical characters were supposed to serve as models for the subordination of women to men.

In order to question biblical prescriptions for human behavior, Stanton had to take a stand against the sacredness of the Bible itself. "The time has come," she said, "to read [the Bible] as we do all other books, accepting the good and rejecting the evil it teaches."[6] In her memoirs, she added, "the more I read, the more keenly I felt the importance of convincing women that the Hebrew mythology had no special claim to a higher origin than that of the Greeks, being far less attractive in style and less refined in sentiment. Its objectionable features would long ago have been apparent had they not been glossed over with a faith in their divine inspiration."[7] Relativizing the Bible by placing it alongside other mythologies as well as "all other books" is a radical step that many feminists both in Stanton's day and in the present are reluctant to take. Many feminists recommend ignoring parts of the Bible, but still claim that the book as a whole is God-given. It is hard to deny that an eventual consequence of criticizing the correctness of any sacred text or tradition is to question why that text or tradition should be considered a divine authority at all. It is to Stanton's credit that she never hedged on this issue.

Many of today's feminists are not yet willing to reject Jewish and Christian tradition at such a basic level. Instead, they turn to exegesis to preserve Jewish and Christian religious systems. They prefer revision to revolution.

One might say that feminist revisionism began with Lucy Stone, another suffragist working in the first wave of American feminism. Stone had been so puzzled by how the Bible was used to malign women that she spent several years learning Greek and Hebrew to discover whether the original texts supported such understandings. Her daughter, Alice, in a biography of her mother, assures us that Stone "always believed and maintained that the Bible, rightly interpreted, was on the side of equal rights for women."[8]

Contemporary feminist critics of religion can be placed on a spectrum ranging from those who revise to those who revolt — from Stone to Stanton — from those who would reform our present stock of images to those who have stopped searching the shelves of the traditional religious warehouses of church, Bible or synagogue and are looking elsewhere. It is important to note that wherever a feminist critic might appear on my spectrum, she is always concerned with problems of imagery. This concern usually expresses itself by attention to questions about the gender of images presented in religious texts and rituals — for example, why many male images are esteemed and why many female images are degraded.

At the present time, most feminist criticism falls at the beginning of my spectrum. Such criticism usually appears in the form of carefully documented essays, articles or books that trace the history of an image or a misogynist tradition to see if it is true, that is, if it is basic to the original text, revelation or custom. I include in this category any work that focuses on a neglected theme, image or practice whether in the major religions, in historical oddities or in sects long defunct. The criticism is characterized by a searching quality, by an effort to address current uneasiness with the answer, "No, this is not basically what real Christianity, Judaism or whatever is about" or by saying, "Look — here is a bit of tradition we can respect, use and expand."

Among the large number of books, articles and essays that typify this reformist genre of feminist work, *Religion and Sexism,* edited by Rosemary Ruether,[9] is the best collection, attempting appraisal and revision of traditional religious themes. I say "best" because the scholarship and documentation of each essay is impeccable. All the writers limit their scope to investigation of a single strand of their Judaeo-Christian heritage and evaluate the material as favorable or unfavorable to women.

Ruether states in her preface that she hopes the book will provide information about the role of the Church in the repression of women. Her own essay, "Virginal Feminism and the Fathers of the Church," does exactly this. At the end of her chapter, the reader is very well informed about how the Church fathers came to idealize the virgin mother of Christ while despising flesh and blood women. In her last paragraph, Ruether suggests that Christianity should "pour [its achievements] back into a full-bodied Hebrew sense of creation and incarnation." She wants Christians to be "fully personalized autonomous selves . . . persons in relation to each other, not against the body, but in and through the body."[10] This suggestion strikes me as impossible. Scorn for the female in general and for the female body in particular is a basic element of Christian practice and symbolism. Though Ruether has hope that Christianity can heal its ideological split between spirit and body, male and female, I fail to see any grounds for optimism.

Ruether does not intend to propose any how-tos and thus should not be criticized for making a far-ranging suggestion without speculating on how it might be implemented. Demanding solid programs for change is often premature and in basic discord with the freedom of thought and action that the women's movement is seeking. However, we should evaluate the directions suggested by present methods of feminist research. The conclusions of a few other essays in *Religion and Sexism* illustrate the precarious position of feminist reformers.

In "Women in the New Testament," Constance Parvey recommends that feminist thought should take its cue from St. Paul's words that there is neither male nor female "in Christ." She hopes to redeem Christianity by claiming that the true way forward is the true way back. Like Ruether, Parvey does not want to say that Christianity cannot be salvaged. She prefers to think that if Christians could return to the message of "primitive Christianity," men and women could be equal. In her work, Parvey recognizes the oppression of women by nearly 2,000 years of Christian misogynist tradition. Nevertheless, she still hopes that it can all be undone. Besides suggesting that

Christians unravel the two millennia of their tradition, she sees no other direction.

In contrast to Parvey, Clara Henning and Bernard Prusak do not argue for religious change on the basis of peripheral strands of Christian tradition. Instead, they see changes in the antifemale bias of the Church as imminent in the face of changing social conditions. Henning, in her article "Canon Law and the Battle of the Sexes," concludes her analysis of sexist practices enshrined in canon law with a warning that "the Church will have less and less to say about this new world unless it can adopt a philosophy that is genuinely equal to the task of speaking about the dignity of humanity — both male and female."[11]

Likewise, Prusak, in his article "Woman: Seductive Siren and Source of Sin?," can find no substantive precedent in Christian theology to justify change in the subordinate status of women. Instead, in a rather despairing tone, he voices some hope for change through secular forces. "It would be unfortunate," he says, "if theologians . . . justified a full *ministerial* role for women only with hindsight . . . when society absolutely required it."[12] Henning and Prusak are both unable to find hope in the Christian doctrines and practices they examined to support future nonsexist practices. Thus, their work suggests no real hope for change from within the tradition.

Judith Hauptman's vision of reform is more paradoxical. In the body of her essay "Images of Women in the Talmud," she goes to great lengths to avoid criticizing rabbinical practice by explaining the social and psychological reasons behind the rabbis' sexist positions. However, at the end of the essay, she calls for a huge overhaul of Talmudic practice. Hauptman wants "all traces of legal and social discrimination against women . . . [to] be discarded." She urges that "[Jewish] women no longer be used as the means with which men achieve their ends."[13] One can only wonder how Jewish law might change, given the massive Talmudic prejudices Hauptman has so carefully outlined. Her work shows a tension between her wish to excuse Judaic patriarchal tradition and to overhaul it radically. If Jewish feminist scholarship does not move beyond this point, work could stagnate for a long time to come.

Although Hauptman's essay provides the most striking example in Ruether's collection of a scholar's ambivalence to her material, the book's other historical essays tend in the same direction. In each case, the writers minimize the patriarchal bias they find in their research by overemphasizing glimmers of dignity granted women within the Jewish and Christian traditions. Their research leads us to the conclusion that even if there was some possibility of freedom and dignity for women in the Jewish and Christian religions, that possibility was continually opposed by Jewish and Christian patriarchs. No matter how carefully the essays in Ruether's collection are worded, we cannot help being impressed with the data these feminist scholars have amassed to show that Judaism and Christianity have always been chiefly concerned with the welfare of males and the exaltation of a male god.

Such careful work does not go far enough. "The pursuit of the past," says feminist historian Sheila Rowbotham, "can become a substitute for trying to change the present. It can become divorced from its original radical impulse and we might find ourselves creating just another academic subject."[14] The world does not need to create "just another academic subject" around cataloguing the details of the degradation of women in Judaism and Christianity. Some feminists need to focus their analytic talents on directions for radical reform so that future religions can be built within nonsexist frameworks. Some of us must have the nerve to go beyond mere research and imagine new possibilities.

In her preface to *Religion and Sexism,* Ruether states

that by "looking back at these [Judaeo-Christian] images [of women], by establishing an autonomous subjectivity from which to study, evaluate and judge these images, women today also shatter this mirror."[15] While it is certainly true that a reappraisal of the past is necessary to arouse our outrage about Jewish and Christian stereotypes of women, fixation on the past will not provide us with forward directions.

To progress toward religions in which new images of women live and thrive we have to make a philosophical leap entirely out of patriarchal structures. One of the ways reformers avoid this rather frightening leap is by retranslating the Bible. In fact, I find the retranslation of Jewish and Christian scripture to be a self-deceptive enterprise. However, since so many feminist thinkers are engaged in this exercise, its approach is worth looking at closely.

A book that typifies this brand of feminist revisionism is *Women and Worship — A Guide to Non-Sexist Hymns, Prayers and Liturgies* by Sharon Neufer Emswiler and Thomas Neufer Emswiler.[16] The book suggests methods for revising the Bible and the Church service in order to alleviate the problem of sexism in Christianity. Sharon Neufer Emswiler begins chapter 1, "How the New Woman Feels in the Old Worship Service," by asking what happens when a worship service fails to inspire, "when the heart fails to function correctly."[17] She describes her alienation as arising from the preponderance of male images surrounding her. The hymns have titles like "Rise Up, O Men of God," "Men and Children Everywhere," and "Faith of Our Fathers." The service contains phrases like "To be is to be a brother." She notices that throughout the service masculine pronouns and adjectives are always used when referring to people or to God. As she leaves the church she asks herself, "Why am I going away feeling less human than when I came?" She answers that "what was meant to be a time of worship of the true God was . . . a worship of the masculine — the masculine experience among humans and the masculine dimension of God."[18] Sharon Emswiler experiences the masculine focus of the Christian service as painful. The images presented by Church personnel and their rituals seem to exclude and even demean her. She tells us that she tries to affirm herself by changing the words of the service in her own mind. But this personal solution does not work well for her. She cannot "out-shout" the rest of the congregation. She wants to have her internal reality — her self-affirmation — confirmed by her surroundings.

Emswiler has experienced alienation from the images that her tradition literally *says* she should find meaningful in a positive fashion. Instead she has felt them to mean negative things. Her response was to write *Women and Worship* with her husband in hopes of altering these images and of experiencing a positive connection with her religious tradition. It is important to note that the impetus to write the book and alter the images comes from her experience in sexist church services. In actual fact, she is treating her private experience as sufficient authority to change sacred scripture and tradition. This is a truly radical move, which Emswiler will not admit even to herself. She quickly backs off from her original impulse in the rest of the book.

Women and Worship goes on to propose detailed reforms both in the church services and in the roles men and women play in such services. The assumption is that such reforms in no way damage the Bible or the Church on any basic level, but rather work within these holy structures to make them more true to their intrinsic sanctity. This assumption is naive.

The authors of *Women and Worship* are uncomfortable about what they are doing. They mention critics who "point out that if we justify editing out the sexism in our Bibles, some other group will want to edit out something else, and pretty soon some of the *eternal validity* of the Bible will be erased by groups who have modernized it on this issue and that."[19] The authors claim that editing the sexism out of the Bible "is not changing the real meaning of the words . . . but instead is amplifying the meaning of the original words."[20]

They feel that if the word "amplifying" begins to mean "changing" then pretty soon some of the *eternal validity* of the Bible will be conjured away. The concern for preserving "eternal validity," or similar concepts connoting sacredness, is basic to any critique that purports to be reforming from within Bible and Church. The issue of whether modifying a sacred text on the basis of personal experience does not somehow indicate a re-evaluation of the sacredness of both the text and the experience is not seriously confronted. *Women and Worship* suggests changes in Christian imagery on the basis of experience yet insists that this does not challenge the imagery of Christ in any essential way. The authors refuse to acknowledge that using experience of images to change images presented in texts elevates experience to the level of text. Perhaps it is true that the sacred quality of the text is being weakened; but then it is equally true that the sacred quality of experience is being recognized.

The Emswilers are at the brink of an important insight when they describe what they are doing as "inserting the appropriate changes as we read." "We do this," they say, "in our own imagination as we read passages [of the Bible] for our own study and meditation."[21] The authors realize that the experience of reading scripture is linked with imagination, so that the text undergoes metamorphosis in the mind. What they do not want to see is that when the imagined change is incorporated into official text it is treated as equal to that text. One might even argue that it is being valued more than the text itself, since it is considered sufficient authority to alter the text, while the text is not being used as authority to question the imaginal experience. The Emswilers have gone as far with their thinking as they found comfortable. Perhaps they have stopped short of pursuing their philosophical premises because they fear that such pursuit might lead them beyond the thresholds of authority of the Church and the Bible.

Like the Emswilers, Letty Russell is a feminist who wants to work with traditional sacred texts and within the structure of the traditional Church. However, unlike the Emswilers, Russell explicitly states that she is using contemporary human experience as the authority to affect those texts and doctrines. She has made her philosophy flexible enough to handle some of the implications of such practices. Russell is a pragmatist who gauges the worth of a piece of scripture or a bit of clerical practice on the basis of how it will work toward "human liberation."

Russell's ordination itself was seen to be "disobeying" parts of the Bible and obeying others. At the ceremony one of her professors read Corinthians 14:34, "the women should keep silence in the churches." This passage was contrasted with Thessalonians 5:19, "Don't quench the Spirit."[22] Russell's whole defense of Christianity places heavy emphasis on the spirit. She retranslates, skips over or reinterprets parts of the Bible that do not support human liberation.

Russell speaks of the "courage and energy" required for "the continued struggle to re-examine the entire Christian tradition as it relates to contemporary social experience."[23] Experience is clearly the measure that tests interpretation of the gospel. Although Russell says that this testing is reciprocal — "The actions of the communities are also tested by the Biblical witness to the meaning and purpose of human liberation as part of God's plan for all of the groaning creation"[24] — her work indicates that she would bend "Biblical witness" whenever the necessity of "liberation" seemed to demand it.

In fact, there is something curiously paradoxical about this position. Although Russell is consciously using experience as the yardstick that measures biblical truth, she often justifies this use of experience on the basis of the Bible itself. She appears to be *playing* at the threshold of ecclesiastical authority when she states that "each person is free to choose the particular style that develops out of tradition, education and life experience."[25] But she still says that the Bible and Christian tradition must be used to endorse that freedom. This ambiguous stance is required if a person wants to hold on to the Christian image system. For example, when Russell speaks of radical change, she depicts Jesus Christ as the chief agent for that change and "God's tradition" is spoken of as Christ's vehicle.[26]

There is no deep understanding of myth and symbol in Russell's theology. While concern for imagery surfaces in her concepts of the search of oppressed peoples for a "usable history" that can provide new ways of self-definition,[27] she does not consider how Christian tradition can provide a significant amount of "usable history" for women.

Jesus Christ cannot symbolize the liberation of women. A culture that maintains a masculine image for its highest divinity cannot allow its women to experience themselves as the equals of its men. In order to develop a theology of women's liberation, feminists have to leave Christ and Bible behind them. Women have to stop denying the sexism that lies at the root of the Jewish and Christian religions.

As soon as Jewish and Christian women face the sexist nature of their traditions, they begin to rely more on themselves and less on "Jesus," "Church" or "Bible." "My concern," says Reverend Peggy Ann Way, "is how a woman, deeply rooted in the profoundly theological issues with which women's liberation is involved, is to understand the authority of her ministry."[28] Way points out that no amount of exegesis can redeem the Bible for women. She does not consider her authority as a minister in the church to be "rooted in the Scriptures," but is "open to the possibility that both the Scriptures and the prevailing tone of cultural development deny [her] such authority."[29] Ultimately, Way roots her authority in flexible "experience" and considers herself a "freer servant than many of [her] masculine colleagues."[30] Way has not justified this authority of experience by maneuvering Scripture or by referring to isolated elements of Christian tradition. She represents a reformist position, which departs markedly from traditional religious doctrine. Although Christ still functions as a symbol for Way, she uses her experience as the measure of how that symbol operates. She does not defend this claim with deceptive exegesis.

Way's work provides a clue to discovering where feminists place religious authority when they begin to move away from biblical symbolism. She tells us that the authority of her ministry is essentially based on her own "experience as it has intersected with Scripture, history, myth, the church and people."[31] Her reflection thus moves from the past to the here-and-now, to the "temporal," the "secular" or whatever terminology can describe the point where experience intersects with "people, history and myth." When feminists set up cornerstones for a new theology, the foundations of this theology need grounding in a place more earthly and immediate than those described by the old abstract terminology of transcendence — a place that allows for "experience" to interact with "Scripture, text, myth and history."

In fact, intuition of the need for such a theological space is present in Rosemary Ruether's work on liberation theology. Ruether depicts what she terms "classical religion" as resting on a basic dichotomy. She shows the dichotomy to have several variants — body/soul, sex/celibacy, woman/man and black/white. Ruether realizes that as soon as any form of these dualisms is challenged, the two-sided framework of secular/sacred is itself threatened. She envisions a wholly new understanding of religion, as something both spiritual and somatic — something that joins soul and body. Ruether sees present culture demanding that religion function in everyday life. "People want contemplation and transcendent experience . . . as a dimension of the totality of life . . . not as an exclusive preoccupation."[32]

Ruether often speaks of third world revolution in her work. Taken metaphorically, the selection of the theme of revolution can be seen as an image that functions for Ruether, Russell and other liberation theologians to express the overthrow of hierarchies *within the mind*. Ruether calls for a psychic revolution as well as a political and economic one. She urges us to overturn a system of theology that honors things of the spirit far more than things of the body. She suggests that we put theology within the milieu of daily living — that theology become a palpable entity in our lives and our thinking. Such a suggestion amounts to seeing theology in a more *psychological* sense, to transforming theology from theorizing about a god "out there," to reflecting on forces and values within human senses and feelings.

Several feminist theologians have taken a psychological direction in their work without explicitly acknowledging it. Sallie McFague TeSelle wants to build a theology that will close the gap between mind and body. She suggests the concept of metaphor as a vehicle for this. Metaphorical thinking, she says, opposes the "Cartesian dichotomy between mind and body, objective and subjective." All of TeSelle's metaphors come from Jesus's parables. She believes that "the parables accept the complexity and ambiguity of life as lived here in this world."[33]

Although TeSelle's work deserves applause for showing

how metaphors are intimately connected to daily living, her theory can have only limited application as long as it remains wholly within the Christian framework. The concept of metaphor as a religious phenomenon can have a much wider range than TeSelle has yet permitted it. Feminist analysis requires this because a feminist theology must cease depending on the metaphor of Jesus *him*self.

Feminist theology is on its way to becoming psychology. Realizing this may prove helpful in the current effort to see secular experience in more sacred terms and sacred doctrine as more a part of secular life. Depth psychology can tie together diverse strands of feminist work in religion and help advance the healing of the split between mind and body.

Although other religious thinkers have attempted to build bridges between the great beyond and the here-and-now, this task compels feminist theologians more than theorists of past generations. Concepts of the "beyond," the "ultimate," the "transcendent" and the "universal" are more important to women since females have been identified with the negative opposites of these terms. Because women have been despised historically as representatives of the "body," the "material" and the "temporal," feminist thought is forced to redeem these concepts.

The distinction between mind and body will begin to wane in Western culture as the women's movement continues to advance. More and more theorists will realize the futility of efforts to reform Judaism and Christianity. Gods who prefer men to women and spirit to body will no longer command respect.

It is likely that as we watch Christ and Yahweh tumble to the ground, we will completely outgrow the need for an external god.

Chapter 3

OEDIPAL PRISONS

NE THEORIST who can help us understand the nature of the religious revolution we are witnessing is Sigmund Freud. Up until very recently, feminists tended to disregard Freud because he continually advised women to *adapt* to their inferior status in patriarchy.[1] Freud, they said, never approved of social revolution; he merely worked to defend existing institutions like the family, patriarchy and capitalism. This observation is certainly true for most of Freud's work. However, it is definitely not true when we look at Freud's thoughts about religion. In the case of religion, Freud called for nothing less than the complete and total overthrow of Judaism and Christianity — and he did this precisely because the religions were patriarchal. His thinking about religion, therefore, is in some ways akin to that of great feminist revolutionary thinkers like Mary Daly. His reasoning not only adds to the twentieth-century indictment of God the Father, but also gives us insight into the sort of human advancement we can expect as our culture undergoes religious revolution.

Freud insisted that God the Father was responsible for keeping huge portions of the human community stupid. He often lamented the intellectual feeble-mindedness a culture that worshiped father-gods instilled in its children. Because no honest testing of religious dogma was permitted, Freud saw religious teaching as harmful to intellectual growth. If people had doubts about religious doctrines they were encouraged to "suppress them, because they thought it was their duty to believe." Freud mourned the "many brilliant intellects [that] have broken down over this conflict" and the "many characters [that] have been impaired by the compromises with which they have tried to find a way out."[2]

The religious thought-control that Freud observed was enforced by the father-gods of Judaism and Christianity. His reconstruction of the primitive origins of all religions is an attempt to explain the contemporary obsession of Christians and Jews with male gods.

In *Totem and Taboo,* Freud says that this religious obsession began with the murder of a primal father by a horde of brothers who desired possession of the women of the tribe. Freud evidently believed that this deed actually happened. "An essential part of the construction," he stated, "is the hypothesis that the events occurred to all primitive men — that is, to all our ancestors."[3]

Religion, according to Freud, is a system of codified reactions to the murder of the father. The reactions alternate between celebration of the killing and deep remorse for the act. Celebration entails rituals of feasting and permissiveness, while remorse generates elaborate taboos around almost everything connected with the memory of the father and his reign.

The role of the father and his relationship to the sons are Freud's themes in both his major works on the history of religions, *Totem and Taboo* (1913) and *Moses and Monotheism* (1939). In the later book, Freud treated Christianity and Judaism as a single tradition forever involved with the problem of the murder of the father. Although Christianity started out as an attempt at "reconciliation with God the Father, atonement for the crime committed against him," Freud pointed out that "the son, who had taken the atonement on himself, became a god himself beside the father and, actually, in place of the father." "Christianity," he continued, "having arisen out of a father-religion became a son-religion. It [did] not [however] escape the fate of having to get rid of the father."[4] Thus we can see that Freud's presentation of Western religious history was exclusively an attempt at explaining the interplay of fathers and sons in contemporary churches and synagogues.

Freud's refusal to recognize the importance of a female presence in religious evolution has enraged many feminists. Eva Figes construes Freud's cursory treatment of mother-goddesses as a sign of his ignorance of the significance of female deities. For Freud, mother-goddesses originated as imagistic recompense for the slighting of real mothers when matriarchy was curtailed. This slight, Freud says, was incurred when the sons recovered from initial guilt over their patricide and assumed the reins of power which they had left in the hands of women for a brief time.[5] For this reason the presence of female deities in religious history can only be an "interesting problem of detail."[6] Figes finds this unacceptable. "Freud," she says, "would have us believe that goddesses were invented as a form of compensation to aggrieved ladies. This is nonsense; goddesses, like all deities, embody authority and belief."[7] But Figes's objection that Freud erred in paying so little attention to images of a feminine godhead is ill-considered. *There are no goddesses in Judaism and Christianity,* the two religions whose pathology Freud was concerned with explaining.

We must remember that Freud framed hypotheses about the primitive history of religions only to explain the construction of present-day Judaism and Christianity — a construction most certainly characterized by its focus on men and male images of God. Freud ignored women because the two religions he was studying showed no major interest in females, whether on earth or in heaven. When Freud looked at Judaism and Christianity he saw only a father-god influencing the behavior of sons. We might criticize him for constructing a historically inaccurate "just-so story"[8] about the patricide to explain the heavy emphasis on father worship. However, we cannot say that he described Judaism and Christianity inaccurately. Freud was not a historian of religion nor was he an anthropologist. He was a medical doctor concerned with mental aberrations. When he looked at Judaism and Christianity, he saw what he judged to be an abnormal obsession by men with father figures whom they imagined to be gods. To explain such an obsession Freud attempted to construct a case history of the religions. Even if his case history of Judaism and Christianity proves inaccurate, his descriptions of father obsession in their doctrines and rituals are still valid and deserve our close attention.

Freud expresses nothing but contempt for Judaism and Christianity in all his writings about their effects on contemporary society. To Freud, religions that worshiped a father-god were the most oppressive institutions in modern culture. In essay after essay Freud inveighed against religions-of-the-father for working to stunt human intellects and for encouraging people to stagnate in Oedipal dependency. For Freud the very word *religion* refers only to belief systems that envision God as a father. He expressed great impatience with "philosophers" whom, he thought, tried to "rescue the God of religion by replacing him [with] an impersonal, shadowy and abstract principle."[9] Freud understood that God is a man no matter how much theologians try to veil "His" sex. He said that he wanted to address theologians with the warning words, "Thou shall not take the name of the Lord thy God in vain!"[10] Freud believed that only by recognizing God for what He was could humanity overcome the crippling dependency inflicted by Him. The father-god kept human beings in the childish state of reliance on external authority by compelling belief and suppressing doubt. A culture that promoted such a God discouraged all aspirations to intellectual strength and freedom. It is clear that Freud believed Judaism and Christianity made people stupid.

Specifically, Freud accused Judaism of preventing intellectual advancement by enforcing an ever-increasing number of rules and customs on functions of everyday life. The rituals with which Jewish people surround their lives were pitiful in Freud's eyes. He likened such behavior to that of obsessive neurotics who are trying to block certain thoughts from consciousness.[11] These rules, Freud insisted, perpetuated the guilt connected with the patricide.[12] Christianity received equal censure for veiling the patricide with the obscure concept of original sin.[13] Belief in original sin prevented people from recognizing the source of the religious injunctions that fostered feelings of guilt. By mystifying people about the nature of God, Christianity became "a severe inhibition upon the intellectual development of the next two thousand years."[14]

Even if we discount Freud's hypothesis about patricide, we still have to acknowledge that his descriptions of Judaism and Christianity are correct. Judaism does tend to restrict life and experience with religious regulations attributed to God or to His male sages. And Christianity does tend to discourage clear thinking about the irrationalities in the life of its male God. In both religions, truly free critical thought about the father-god and his son is forbidden.

In his early writings, fear of censure softened Freud's attack on Judaism and Christianity. As he grew older, his criticisms became more direct. The Jewish and Christian versions of the father-god functioned as severe detriments to human progress. In order for humankind to advance along more promising lines, the father would have to be dethroned.

Freud's analysis of why fixation on father images damages both a person's intellectual scope and his or her ability to make valuable contributions to society lies in his understanding of the Oedipal complex. Whether one is fixated on one's real father or on God the Father, such preoccupation will hamper growing up. In Freudian terms *growing up* means growing out of the Oedipal complex in which authority is imagined as an external father figure. When a man or woman is no longer obsessed with the father, he or she develops a sense of internal authority that can be relied upon to guide thought and feeling. Freud named this internal authority the *superego* and thought individuals who had developed superegos were great assets to any society. With a healthy superego, a person could accept the demands of life and function rationally and creatively. However, if the superego was not properly developed, the individual would not be able to move so freely in the world. He or she would be either overly strict and authoritarian or excessively irresponsible and childlike. Freud attributed both extremes to superegos crippled by fixation on the father. Judaism and Christianity were forces which kept vast numbers of people handicapped in regard to superego development.

Freud was specifically concerned with how Judaism and Christianity weakened the intellects of men. He believed that "when a man has once brought himself to accept uncritically all the absurdities that religious doctrines put before him and even to overlook the contradictions between them, we need not be greatly surprised at the weakness of his intellect."[15] Freud thought women's minds were more likely to be stunted by early prohibition of thinking about sex. "Intellectual atrophy" among women, he speculated, was probably brought on by "the harshness of an early prohibition against turning their thoughts to what would most have interested them — namely, the problems of sexual life."[16]

Although Freud did not address the issue of how father religions specifically affected the intellects of women, his theories can be used to speculate on an interesting possibility. Freud's writings point to this conclusion: *Religions chiefly concerned with fathers and sons work greater harm on the intellects of women since such religions make resolution of the Oedipal complex even more difficult for women than it would normally be.* A review of Freud's thinking on Oedipal development supports this intriguing hypothesis.

Though Freud at first found no difference between men and women in their resolution of the Oedipal complex, his researches gradually led him to another conclusion. In 1923 he wrote that the process of the development of masculinity in boys and of femininity in girls was "precisely analogous" vis-à-vis their Oedipal situations.[17] A year later he began to doubt this conclusion. He admitted that the psychological development of girls confused him. "The Oedipal process," which he had described, he said, "refers to male children only. How does the corresponding development take place in little girls? At this point our material for some incomprehensible reason becomes far more obscure and full of gaps."[18] In the same paper Freud noted that in little girls a "powerful motive . . . for the setting-up of a super-ego" was absent because they had no fear of castration.[19] Since little girls had no fear of being castrated as punishment for their incestuous feelings, they had less emotional impetus to grow out of those feelings than had boys. Thus little girls were likely to stay in the Oedipal situation of involvement with the father for a longer time. Their superegos suffered for it. Freud attributed a great deal to the weak superegos of women:

I cannot evade the notion (though I hesitate to give it expression) that for women the level of what is ethically normal is different from what it is in men. Their super-ego is never so impersonal, so independent of its emotional origins as we require it to be in men.

Character-traits which critics of every epoch have brought up against women — that they show less sense of justice than men, that they are less ready to submit to the great exigencies of life, that they are more often influenced in their judgments by feelings of affection or hostility — all these would be amply accounted for by the modification in the formation of their super-ego. . . . We must not allow ourselves to be deflected from such considerations by the denials of the feminists.[20]

I suggest that feminists not be "deflected" from consideration of Freud's observation of the problems women have in resolving their Oedipal complex because of his agreement with the "critics of every epoch" about the defective character traits of women. It is more important to note that for Freud worthwhile people were adults with strong superegos. Remaining caught in the Oedipal dynamic meant stagnating in childish dependency on the father. Both feminists and Freud are in agreement on the fact that childish reliance on males does not enhance women's ability to contribute as adults to the work of culture. In Freud's language, the girl entered the Oedipal situation when she transferred what he termed her wish for a penis to her father. Her lack of "castration anxiety" made it difficult for her to grow out of this phase and her development was likely to be stunted far into adult life.

We do not have to accept all of Freud's terms to see the significance of his theory. Feminist theorists have understood that instead of transferring their wish for a penis to their fathers, the little girls Freud was watching were transferring their wish for social power to their fathers.[21] In fact, female transference of any wish to fathers constitutes a serious problem in the self-development of many women. Stagnation in the Oedipal situation happens whenever women project their desire for independence and prestige on to men. Such projection prevents women from living out these desires in their own lives.

In his last remark on the subject, Freud speculated that perhaps the more complicated Oedipal situation of women did not always work to their detriment. Toward the end of his life, Freud seemed to have decided that remaining in the Oedipal complex could benefit women since they would be more likely to accept the "authority" of their husbands. "It does little harm to a woman," he said, "if she remains in her feminine Oedipus attitude. . . . She will in that case choose her husband for his paternal characteristics and be ready to recognize his authority. Her longing to possess a *penis* [understand power], which is in fact unappeasable, may find satisfaction if she can succeed in completing her love of the organ by extending it to the bearer of the organ."[22]

In this last remark about the implications of an unresolved Oedipal complex in women, Freud did not mention the consequences of an underdeveloped superego on the female character. Instead, he seems rather sanguine about the matter. If one recognized the fact that many women would always remain caught in the Oedipal complex, and if one did not care about harm this would do to the formation of their superegos, one could be consoled by thinking how this very stagnation could allow women to accept their subordinate roles as wives.

While Freud did not deal with the subject directly, it is worth speculating what he might have thought about the consequences for women implied by a father religion. His writings suggest two answers. It could be that the predominance of father worship in religion would not be detrimental for women. Participation in religious practices based on the Oedipal dynamic might be one more pressure on women to remain fixated to males and thus to accept the authority of their husbands.

Another answer is possible, however. If Freud had been concerned only about the blocks in the development of a superego in women, he might well have thought that father worship in religion could only add another burden to the female sex, making a woman's possible contribution to intellectual and cultural life even more difficult. Freud might have thought that participating in a father religion would be an added handicap to a woman's attainment of psychological independence and thus severely inhibit her reaching the psychological ideal he called "the primacy of the intelligence."[23] Judaism and Christianity could only hamper further the attainment of this ideal, since the doctrines of these religions stressed dependence on the authority of the fathers. For women, such religious teaching could only add greater difficulty to their already complicated Oedipal situation. Under the reign of father religions, Freud might have thought that women had less chance to participate significantly in intellectual culture.

However, whether Freud would have thought so or not is purely speculative. My major point is that Freud's work on religion and the Oedipal complex indicates that religion based on father worship is certainly not conducive to the psychological independence of women. Whether or not we decide that Freud would have agreed that such psychological independence was either possible or beneficial for the female sex, it is certain that he did not see fixation on the Oedipal complex as fostering such independence. In this sense Freudian thought supports a basic conviction of current feminist theory: for women to become intellectually responsible and creative members of society, they have to outgrow Oedipal dependence on paternal authority whether that authority is embodied in a paternalistic husband, or father or God.

Freud's Oedipal theory leads us to see how important the demise of Yahweh and Christ is to the intellectual independence of Western women. Freud was certain that Judaism and Christianity stunted the intellectual maturity of men. It is probable, however, that these religions are even more damaging to the intellectual growth of women. By picturing ultimate authority as a paternal male, Judaeo-Christian culture is greatly compounding the difficulties women already have in emerging from their Oedipal dependence and accepting responsibility for their own lives.

When we contemplate the fall of the great father-gods, we are contemplating the eradication of Oedipal religions. Freud had hoped that psychoanalysis would eliminate father-gods through scientific reasoning. But, in fact, feminism may prove to be more effective. By challenging the authority of males on earth, feminists make effective onslaughts on male authority in heaven. The feminist attack is probably more basic than the one made by Freud. Freud's insistence on male rule in the family and in society does not challenge the image people have of authority itself as paternal. Freudian theory still gives real authority to males even though it argues against projecting that authority to an external supernatural realm. Feminism, on the other hand, challenges male authority at the basic imagistic level. The feminist quarrel with the male nature of God is readily understandable to millions who could never follow Freudian logic. People who could never comprehend Oedipal theory can easily understand that if men are no longer the sole rulers of earth, it makes no sense at all to leave them in charge of heaven. The women's movement is destined to spread religious revolution in levels of popular culture that psychoanalysis could never reach. If Freud was right about the stultifying effect of father-gods on human energy, then when the feminist movement succeeds in toppling Yahweh and Christ, it will succeed in freeing millions of men and women from the psychological tyranny of Oedipal prisons. Vast amounts of human energy will be liberated.

Chapter 4

WHEN FATHERS DIE

WE ALL TURN INWARD

WE ARE about to learn what happens when father-gods die for an entire culture.

Since all recorded history has been patriarchal, there are no written records to help us predict how institutional forms will change when society grants public authority to both sexes. However, we do know a lot about what happens to individuals when their fathers die, or, to put it more accurately, what happens to individuals when their fathers' authority over them is no longer effective. As we have seen, the experience of overcoming dependence on our fathers fascinated Sigmund Freud. Freud's thoughts on the death of fathers provide insight into the eclipse of masculine authority in Western culture as a whole. We can also learn from what we ourselves experience regarding our own fathers and from what others tell us about their growing up. About ten years ago, I dreamed that my father died. I was terrified. Although my father was in perfect health, I was terrified by the sense of reality of this dream. It bothered me for years afterward — and I was often prompted to make long-distance telephone calls to ask about the state of my father's health. I greatly feared the death of my father and was afraid that my dream was a portent.

My dream was indeed portentous. It was not, however, a prediction of my father's actual death. I became anxious about my father's death at the time when I was beginning to take control of my own life — when I was beginning to rely on my own judgment about more and more aspects of living. Like most women, I did not feel very confident about directing my own life and was eager to place myself under the care and tutelage of father figures — figures like male professors and male psychoanalysts. (Other women may have chosen male clergymen, representing male gods, as substitutes for the father.)

The dream of the death of my father was an accurate image of what was really happening to me. Although I was resisting the change, the authority of men was beginning to have less power over me. But because this seemed so unnatural and because I was so frightened of relying on myself — the dream was terrifying. It continued to disturb my sleep until I grew up, that is, until I had come to feel that a life without a man controlling it was all right. About the same time that the dream stopped recurring I became increasingly introspective and much more interested in my own dreams and fantasy images. For me, the dream of my father's death was the beginning of a psychological movement inward.

Just recently, I watched another woman begin a similar process. I met Charlotte at a summer institute for language training in Germany. She was a nineteen-year-old English woman who had never been away from home. After about a week of living on her own, she began to have a recurring dream about her father's death. It was the first dream she ever remembered having. The dream troubled her very much even though her own father was in perfect health. Apparently, the experience of living independently was killing off Charlotte's psychological reliance on her father. The fact that her father's death was the first dream to affect her consciously showed that the death of Charlotte's psychic father was spurring her to become more aware of her own mental life. She began to remember more and more dreams as the summer progressed. I felt sure that the content of Charlotte's first dream was related to the growth of her power both to live alone and to become more observant about her dream processes.

A decrease in dependence on her father seems to go hand in hand with an increase in a woman's awareness of her own needs and feelings. In her autobiography, artist Judy Chicago tells us about the effects of the early death of her father.[1] By the time she had reached her mid-twenties, she had lost both her father and her husband, who, she tells us, was the "intellectual reflection" of her father.[2] She went through a good deal of psychotherapy to unravel her feelings about their deaths. Thus Chicago painfully learned to accept both the physical and psychological loss of two powerful men in her life. After working through these tragedies, she developed a vibrant artistic style, deriving her images from her own body and emotions. Her paintings and sculptures are expressions of her intense awareness of her own physical and psychic presence. I do not think that Chicago could produce such imagery if she had not first freed herself so completely from reliance on male authority. Although Judy Chicago remarried and did not cut all bonds with men, delving into her relations with male authority figures and severing the ties to those figures enabled her to be free enough to explore womanhood extensively in her art. For Judy Chicago, freedom from father meant freedom to dive deep within herself and there to find sources of strength and inspiration.

Intense focus on oneself after the death of a father is by no means unique to women. Heightened introspection after the loss of a male authority figure occurred in the lives of both Carl Jung and Sigmund Freud. When Jung and Freud broke off their relationship, Jung lost contact with a formidable father figure. It was "a period of inner uncertainty," Jung wrote, "a state of disorientation. . . . I felt totally suspended in mid-air, for I had not yet found my own footing."[3] Jung withdrew into himself for no less than six years. During this time he "confronted the unconscious" — an experience which he describes extensively in his autobiography. Jung was forced to look into himself to continue functioning in the world. He emerged from his private, difficult journey with a wealth of material about the way dreams, fantasies, myths and images function in the mind. In regaining his footing, Jung discovered the direction of his entire life's work.

When his father died, Sigmund Freud began work on *The Interpretation of Dreams,* an exhaustive study of both dreams in general and Freud's own dreams in particular. Freud said the book constituted a "portion of my own self-analysis, my reaction to my father's death — that is to say, to the most important event, the most poignant loss of a man's life."[4] Thus Freud's own exploration of the deep life of the mind began in earnest when his father died.

Perhaps the loss of one's father — whether through physical death of the father or through psychological growth away from his authority — is an event that generally precedes serious introspection. In our culture we usually feel on more intimate terms with our mothers, the parent who cares for our bodily needs when we are infants. We experience our fathers as someone distant from us, someone who represents rules and forces outside ourselves.[5] When fathers die in a psychological sense, the powers we imagine as external to us lose a good deal of their mystique. We are thrown into ourselves to seek the bases for our own lives. Feelings that someone or something "out there" has the rules for "proper" living tend to vanish.

My scenario here is far too sketchy, however. Further

study and reflection are necessary to examine the process of turning inward that individuals experience when their fathers lose authority. In fact, this is just the sort of theorizing that must be done as we attempt to imagine what will happen when father-gods die. One can say at this point: *since introspection does follow the death of fathers, then the death of father-gods could mean the onset of religious forms which emphasize awareness of oneself and tend to understand gods and goddesses as inner psychic forces.*

Freud wanted psychoanalysis to put a complete end to the belief that mythological and religious entities had any existence apart from the human psyche. In 1901 he made a comment that has profound implications for the question — "What will happen to God?" Freud said:

In point of fact I believe that a large part of the mythological view of the world, which extends a long way into the most modern religions, *is nothing but psychology projected into the external world.* The obscure recognition of psychical factors and relations in the unconscious is mirrored . . . in the construction of a supernatural reality, which is destined to be changed back once more by science into the psychology of the unconscious. One could venture to explain in this way the myths of paradise and fall of man, of God, of good and evil, of immortality, and so on.[6]

Freud predicted that what we once conceived of as religion would someday be thought of as "psychology." We will come to understand that God the Father, Christ and Adam and Eve are all representations of wishes and conflicts — that, in fact, they exist in the mind and nowhere else. Psychology will eventually convince humanity that all myths, whether founded in the dogma of contemporary religions or in the plots of ancient literature, have their bases in the mind and should never be credited with a reality independent of the mind.

There is a pejorative word for the philosophical movement I am discussing. That word is "reductionist." Many thoughtful people feel that placing religion in the mind represents a refusal to understand religion on its own terms. Seeing religion as an internal psychic phenomenon, they say, is an attempt to make it conform to the alien framework of psychology. They argue that moving religion into the mind minimizes the importance of sacred experience and *reduces* it to something less grand, that is, to activities of human mental life.

There has always been a general feeling that a psychological perspective debunks and debases religious truth. The following passage from *Looking for Mr. Goodbar* illustrates how reduction can operate in popular thought about religion. In this sequence, Theresa is asking her lover, James, to talk about his severely paralyzed mother.

"What is she like, your mother?"
"She is a very sweet person," he said. "She always was. Sweet, quiet, somewhat stoical. Of course being helpless has tended to . . . she's very religious. She prays a great deal. There's no doubt in my mind that belief in God and the hereafter has kept her from going mad."
"Do you still believe in God?"
He smiled. "How could I not believe in the God who's kept my mother from going mad?"
"You might believe in Him as a force in your mother's mind without believing in Him as a reality."[7]

Theresa is expressing contempt for James, his mother and God when she refers to God as a "force in your mother's mind." She is not, however, questioning the efficacy of his mother's belief in God. This is the paradox of the reductionist position. Although religious beliefs are seen as existing only in the mind, they are still credited with impact and psychic reality. For some people, this position is highly damaging to the religious experience. These people need to think of gods and religious feelings as having a reality external to human beings. Many people can not respect religious entities if they think of those entities as existing only in the mind.

Another view is possible, however. Why should locating myths and religious beliefs within a mental or psychic milieu diminish those beliefs to any great extent? After all, the reality of the human mind is extremely important. If something exists as a force in the mind, it is deserving of attention and analysis. Perhaps the worst thing the mind can do is deceive itself about the internal nature of its experience. In psychoanalysis, the most important factor is the recognition of the forces and complexes that operate to structure one's experience. Such recognition allows a person to live in better relation to his or her basic nature. The fact that mental forces are in fact *mental* forces does not minimize their significance for human life.

Why should we feel that the God of James's mother is any less powerful because that power resides in her mind? We feel this way because we, in Western culture, have placed a great deal of value on forces of comfort and salvation thought of as outside ourselves. It is possible, that as psychological thinking becomes more familiar to us, seeing a god or other mythical being as a force within the mind will not diminish the importance of that being to any appreciable extent. We could still experience the full effects of religious imagery within the mind even though we no longer accord that imagery reality outside the mind.

Paradoxically, although Freud saw psychoanalysis as the enemy of *all* religion, it may prove to be merely the enemy of a religion which pretends existence outside the mind. Psychoanalytic method and philosophy actually promote religious notions of gods and powers that are internal. Freud himself came close to admitting this in the case of mysticism.

Freud believed that some mystical procedures had merit because, like psychoanalysis, they led to exploration of deep levels of the mind. Given Freud's utter contempt for any other religious practices, his curiosity about mysticism is worth noting. "It is easy to imagine . . . ," he said, "that certain mystical practices may succeed in upsetting the normal relations between the different regions of the mind so that, for instance, perception may be able to grasp happenings in the depths of the ego and in the id which were otherwise inaccessible to it."[8] Freud was quite explicit in denying that the effects of mysticism could lead to any grand sort of redemption. "It may safely be doubted," he said, "whether this road will lead us to the ultimate truths from which salvation is to be expected. . . . *Nevertheless,*" he added, "*it may be admitted that the therapeutic efforts of psychoanalysis have chosen a similar line of approach* [italics mine]. [Psychoanalysis'] intention is, indeed, to strengthen the ego, to make it independent of the super-ego, to widen its field of perception and enlarge its organization, so that it can appropriate fresh portions of the id."[9]

We see, then, that the similarity Freud saw between psychoanalysis and mysticism lay in the focus of both on the interior of the human mind. Mysticism was on Freud's mind right up to the end of his life. Four days before he died, Freud wrote in his journal that "mysticism is the obscure self-perception of the realm outside the ego, of the id."[10] Psychoanalysis and mysticism are both avenues to the id.

Whether we reach satisfying and reliable truths about internal experience through mysticism or psychoanalysis is relatively unimportant. It is far more important whether or not we consider the activity of probing the major forces in our minds as a valuable activity. When we think of experiencing God, gods or myths as forces in the mind, we ought to question the charge that this is merely a reductive method for refuting a belief. The location of a god in the mind may be the most effective place that she, he or it can be in an age of post-Oedipal culture.

If it is indeed true that religious sensibility turns inward when father-gods fall, then the thinkers who should now be able to give us insights are those who have been concerned with religious experiences within the human mind. In the following pages I will explore philosophies and contemporary movements that focus on the internal nature of religious awareness. As I look at the radical theories and practices of our new era, I will mingle descriptions of what *is* with concerns of what *ought to be*. In this time of tremendous social and philosophic change, one of the most worthwhile activities is to dream about the best course these changes can take. While we may not have much control over changes in the whole of humanity, we can certainly gain direction for construction of our own personal religious consciousness.

Chapter 5

JUNGIAN PSYCHOLOGY AND RELIGION

PSYCHOLOGIST Carl Jung has given us this century's most significant work on the exploration of religious processes within the human mind. Unlike Freud, Jung thought that psychoanalysis could gain a great deal from adopting a religious standpoint.

Jung and Freud had their first recorded argument about religion in 1910. Freud had been approached by a Swiss pharmacist named Knapp about joining a new organization, Internationaler Orden für Ethik und Kultur. Freud was very interested and wrote to friends to ask their advice. "What attracted me," he wrote, "was the practical, aggressive as much as protective, feature of the program: the obligation to fight directly against the authority of the State and the Church in cases where they are committing manifest injustice."[1]

We can see that Freud was attracted to the ethical concerns of the organization. When he wrote to Jung, he expressed excitement over the idea of combining morality with psychoanalysis. He asked Jung to join the group with him. "If we join," he said, "we shall be able to draw the moralists to psychoanalysis rather than let the psychoanalysts be turned into moralists."[2] Surprisingly, Jung's reply was an emphatic no.

Jung did not want psychoanalysis to have any relation to an organization concerned with ethics and morality.

"I imagine," he told Freud, "a far finer and more comprehensive task for psychoanalysis than alliance with an ethical fraternity. I think we must give it time to infiltrate into people from many centres, to revivify among intellectuals a feeling for symbol and myth."[3] He asked Freud, "What sort of myth does this organization hand out for us to live by? Only the wise are ethical from sheer intellectual presumption, the rest of us need the eternal truth of myth. . . . Religion," Jung said, "can only be replaced by religion."[4]

We see, then, that Jung wanted psychoanalysis to take on the revivification of myth. To accomplish this, he believed, one did not use an ethical alliance. Jung suggested that psychoanalysis set itself up as a new sort of religion — that psychoanalysis teach people how to live by "myth." This was the only way, he told Freud, that psychoanalysis could effectively combat 2,000 years of Christianity.

The most important feature of any religion is its myth. By myth, Jung meant much more than story or illusion. When Jung used the word myth he referred to the deepest sort of experience in human life. Mythic images are indeed pictures. However, they are pictures that involve us both physiologically in our bodily reactions to them and spiritually in our higher thoughts about them. When a person is aware of living mythically, she or he is experiencing life intensely and reflectively. Such people experience life as meaningful. "Meaning" in psychoanalysis is a subjective state.

A number of years ago, I was arguing with a friend, a psychoanalyst, that life was meaningless. I told him there was no purpose, no ideal, no ideology he could name that I could not debunk as being ultimately meaningless. He agreed. However, he pointed out that psychoanalysis understood meaning as a feeling — even as a sensation. A person experienced meaning whether or not she or he could defend the experience against all conceivable philosophic onslaughts. Meaning, he thought, resulted from a sense of reality or tangibility about the life one was leading. I saw his point. Although meaning can never be proven in any absolute way, it can be seen operating in the lives of people.

If people lead lives that are somehow incorrect for them, they experience "loss of meaning" or "loss of reality." A meaningless life is one of disconnection. Whatever you feel to be you does not resonate very much with the things "you" are doing. Adjustments are needed to build bridges between the two. Myths function as the building materials of reality. They connect mind and body, matter and spirit, people and their experience. This connection is vivid and palpable. The value of a myth is judged by the quality of the interior feeling it generates in individuals.

The function of religions, Jung believed, is to provide people with myths to live by. Since religions seem to be increasingly unable to fulfill this task in modern times, Jung thought it was up to psychology to reacquaint people with myths. In other words, it was up to psychology to become religion. Jung criticized the theories of Freud and Adler because "their exclusive concern with the instincts fails to satisfy . . . deeper spiritual needs."[5] Freudian and Adlerian psychology gave "too little value to fictional and imaginative processes," Jung said. "In a word, they do not give enough meaning to life. And it is only meaning that liberates."[6]

Jung set out to build a psychology that would function like religion. This psychological religion was designed for any person who had "outgrown" the "local form of religion" she or he had been "born into."[7] It was a religion for doubters, for people who were critical of the standardized institutional religions of their culture and yet who felt a need for religious reflection. Thus Jung defined his "patients."

Jung tells us that most of his patients did not have trouble coping with everyday life. Instead, they suffered from sicknesses of the soul — from experiences of meaninglessness and confusion. As an analyst, he felt his job was to revivify a sense of myth within these people. If there was a chance of re-establishing a link with the person's native religion, Jung encouraged a return to the original faith. When this was impossible, that is, when the patient saw too many faults in her or his native religion, then Jung had the more difficult task of guiding the person to discover a religious process within the self.

Jung's importance for feminist thinking lies in the methods he devised to cure religious alienation. As more and more of society accepts feminist criticism of patriarchal religious systems, more and more people will be seeking alternative religious forms. We have seen that when father-gods fall, people tend to look inward to understand the forces or gods that are at work in their lives. Since Jung pioneered the psychological search for religious forces, his work becomes increasingly relevant in the post-Oedipal age.

IN SEARCH OF A LIVING RELIGION

True religion has to be alive. This life consists in how well the religion nurtures a mythic understanding in its followers. Catholicism, for example, almost qualifies as living religion because it presents the rich imagery of the story of Jesus and the lives of the saints. All of the ceremony, ritual, mystery and color of Catholic tradition provides many Catholics with a vital mythic context in which to live. However, even though Catholicism has myth and mystery, it is a dying religion.

Catholicism, Jung observed, can not allow individual people to depart from the myths dispensed by the Catholic hierarchy. Thus, if someone needs to reflect on images other than those presented by Jesus, she or he is vigorously discouraged from doing so. The person is made to feel guilty and sinful if her or his psychic experience differs appreciably from that of Jesus. In past times, Catholicism dispensed with people with different visions by labeling them heretics. What is a *heretic* if not someone who experiences religious consciousness in myths other than those prescribed by tradition? If a religion allows no room for its heretics, it leaves no room for individuals who need to live their own myths. Catholicism is fine for obedient souls — for those whose imaginations could fit into standardized categories. The creators, however, have to leave the faith.

Jung romanticized creators to a great extent. He viewed himself and many of his patients as part of an elite cadre, set apart from the herd, whose psyches were too original to fit into stereotyped molds. He dwelt very little on the possibility that more and more people would find themselves playing the role of religious creator. When the stereotyped molds of Catholic experience are smashed by the awareness of sexism, an increasing number of people will become heretics of tradition. Their need for new myths will be unable to be filled by prescriptions derived from an imitation of Christ. Jung's criticism of Catholicism might become the "daily bread" of millions who, although they may never hear of Jung, will perceive a deadness in Catholic mythology.

Some features of Protestantism make it better qualified to endure in an age with an increasing demand for living religion. Protestantism has purged itself of most myth, ritual and imagery. Jung saw it becoming increasingly undogmatic with fewer and fewer mythic models to force on its followers. Protestantism seems to be developing a greater tolerance for variety both in individuals and in sects. In this sense, it permits a person to explore her or his experience more freely than does Catholicism.

However, even though Protestantism is generally good-natured about permitting people to go their own way, it offers no insights into the nature of myth. Protestantism gives its followers no clues about what living a life informed by myth and symbol might mean. While Catholicism presents a standardized set of myths to live by, Protestantism offers nothing at all. It is likely that Protestants will have a harder time constructing a living religion since they have little training in recognizing religious imagery.

The range of Jung's criticism of Protestantism and Catholicism applies to all the world's major faiths. If a religion such as orthodox Judaism presented a rich tradition of myth and ritual to its followers, Jung would approve of the type of experience the religion offered; nevertheless, he would criticize it for not allowing individuals to discover their own myths. On the other hand, if a religion such as Quakerism allowed much latitude to its followers, Jung would be pleased by the absence of dogma, yet dismayed by the lack of substantial mythic content. Both kinds of religion fail to be truly alive.

What then is a living religion? It is a religion that satisfies a person's need for mythic reflection and understanding. Technically, any standardized religious system can be "alive" for a person as long as it coincides with her or his specific needs for myth and image. The more aware a person is of her or his individuality, however, the less likely is a standardized religious package to suffice.

Christ, Buddha, Mohammed and all other founders of traditions have experienced living religion. They have lived their lives in uncompromising loyalty to their visions, that is, to their myths. Disciples are so impressed by the stature of these leaders — by the force and power devotion to their visions conferred upon them — that they found mythic systems based on the content of the leader's experience. The myths of the leaders, however, never have the same impact on the disciples. Jung believed it was the *process* of discovery of the myth that gave the leaders their power. Without going through a similar process, a disciple could not experience the original myth. Appropriation of the content of the founder's vision could not make the vision work in the way it did for the founder; power was lost. Unless the disciple discovered her or his own vision, pale imitation of the leader was all that was possible.

There is a story that illustrates this point very well. A wise woman went into a cave to meditate. She stayed there for many years, drawing all sorts of diagrams on the walls to solve the mystery of life. Finally, she drew an elliptical shape with purple chalk and added a yellow triangle in the middle. "I have solved the mystery of life," she said and left the cave to resume her previous way of life. People from all parts of the district flocked to the cave. They saw the yellow triangle inside the purple ellipse and copied it down. "Now I have the answer to life," each one exclaimed. This, of course, was not true. In fact, the purple and yellow design had come to the old woman only after years of scrutiny of her own soul. It was the process that she had undergone to discover the figure that had made it the symbol of her solution. The purple ellipse was a myth of great power for the old woman. For her disciples, it was merely a purple ellipse.[8]

Most of us do not choose to live as intensely as the great founders of religions — Christ, Buddha, Mohammed — or even the old woman in the fable. For most of us, standardized religious creeds would do nicely. However, when those creeds become blatantly objectionable, complacency is no longer possible. Today, more and more of us are stuck with the difficult task of making sense of life for ourselves.

HOW DO YOU BUILD A COMMUNITY
IF EVERYONE DOES HER
OR HIS OWN THING?

There is a problem with the concept of living religion. If everyone becomes committed to developing her or his own set of myths and symbols, how is community possible? One of the valuable functions the great religious traditions serve is the unification of large groups of people around a given set of symbols. Christians, Jews and Moslems have sets of rituals which are based on the myths of their sacred texts and function to bring people together for communal acts of joy and sadness, meditation and celebration. Such rituals are possible, one might argue, only if members of a religion acknowledge that they are all somehow alike — that they can all feel the importance of the same set of images and symbols.

It is for this reason, one might say, that we need to maintain standardized sets of religious imagery. Human beings enjoy the feeling of sharing common myths and common histories. If we deny these unifying ties and embark on projects of creating individual myths and symbols, won't we be cutting ourselves off from one of the great pleasures of being human?

I am going to argue that it is not necessary for human beings to share the *same* myths, images and symbols. Instead, it is more important that human beings share the *process* of symbol creation itself. This is an age in which pluralism is a fact of life. At no other time in history have the ideals of freedom of thought had so much chance to become part of so many facets of social and cultural life. By advocating any restrictive set of myths and images, we will be limiting human experience once again. One of the great ideals of the feminist cultural revolution is that all human beings be encouraged to find their own dignity and pursue their own truth. The creation of a new set of stereotypes would be sad indeed.

In the chapters that follow, I hope to show how sharing

the processes of symbol creation can build a sense of community. Before doing that, however, I want to return to Jung once more — this time for guidance as to what *not* to do in an age of religious innovation.

THOU SHALT NOT CREATE ARCHETYPES!

About four years ago in Zurich, while preparing one of Jung's seminars for publication, I read a statement that appalled me. Jung was making some observations about Africa and said that when one referred to Negroes one was getting very close to the "gorilla." Since direct quotation from Jung's seminars is not permitted, I cannot supply more of his exact words. Nevertheless, I do not see any reason to refrain from mentioning what I read. The comment is unfortunately typical of a dangerous tendency in Jungian thought — the tendency to make sweeping generalizations about the essential nature of races, nationalities and the sexes. Here is a sampling of the type of generalizations Jung made about Americans and blacks. In 1910, Otto Rank summarized a lecture that Jung had given on America. Rank says:

Lecturer described a number of impressions he had gained on two journeys in North America. The psychological peculiarities of the Americans exhibit features that would be accessible to psychoanalysis, since they point to intense sexual repression. The reasons for repression are to be sought in the specifically American complex, namely, living together with lower races, more particularly the Negroes. Living together with barbarous races has a suggestive effect on the laboriously subjugated instincts of the white race and drags it down. Hence strongly developed defensive measures are necessary, which manifest themselves in the particular aspects of American culture.[9]

In 1927 Jung further developed some of these ideas about Americans and blacks in a lecture called "Mind and Earth."

Another thing that struck me [about America] was the great influence of the Negro, a psychological influence naturally, not due to the mixing of blood. The emotional way an American expresses himself, especially the way he laughs, can best be studied in the illustrated supplements of the American papers; the inimitable Teddy Roosevelt laugh is found in its primordial form in the American Negro. The peculiar walk with loose joints, or the swinging of the hips so frequently observed in Americans, also comes from the Negro. American music draws its main inspiration from the Negro, and so does the dance. The expression of religious feeling, the revival meetings, the Holy Rollers and other abnormalities are strongly influenced by the Negro, and the famous American naiveté, in its charming as well as its more unpleasant form, invites comparison with the childlikeness of the Negro.[10]

Jung found the African blacks more threatening than those in America.

This infection by the primitive can . . . be observed just as well in other countries, though not to the same degree and in this form. In Africa, for example, the white man is a diminishing minority and must therefore protect himself from the Negro by observing the most rigorous social forms, otherwise he risks "going black." If he succumbs to the primitive influence he is lost. But in America the Negro, just because he is a minority, is not a degenerative influence, but rather one which, peculiar though it is, cannot be termed unfavourable — unless one happens to have a jazz phobia.[11]

Anyone who admires Jung's work is likely to find these statements embarrassing. Nevertheless, we must recognize the weaknesses of Jung's theory as well as the strengths if we are to utilize his work in this age of religious change. There are several things wrong with Jung's observations about Americans and blacks. He appears to be a naive person who judges other cultures only in terms of his own. Blacks in Africa and in America play the role of primitives for Jung, who obviously sees white European culture as much superior. Furthermore, Jung seems to believe just what he sees. For him blacks *were* childlike and innocent. He does not even wonder if this might not be a pose adopted for survival in racist culture.

I have always been impressed by the ease with which Jung slips into generalizations. In "Mind and Earth" he facilely concludes that blacks have rhythm, are childlike and primitive. Then, on the basis of this observation, he decides that in Africa the white minority must protect themselves from such regression. In America, however, because whites are in the majority, they can afford to be less concerned and simply be amused by the proximity of the musical Negroes.

This tendency to generalize about individuals and then to prescribe behavior appropriate to the generalizations is a serious flaw in Jung's work. Jung often claimed archetypal status for the categories he formulated. Once a description of a national group, of a psychic situation or of either of the two sexes was considered an archetype, it became immune to sociological analysis. It was treated as a universal fact of life, which one simply had to accept. Jung's views on women exhibit the weakness of this archetypal approach.

Jung is often considered to be an ally of the women's movement because of the high value he placed on "the feminine." It is certainly true that he thought women who exhibited the feminine deserved more respect in Western culture. However, as soon as a woman began to behave in a way that deviated from Jung's feminine archetypes, she was heavily censured. For example, Jung believed that women courted psychological disaster if they attempted to work at "masculine" jobs:

No one can get around the fact that by taking up a masculine profession, studying and working like a man, woman is doing something not wholly in accord with, if not directly injurious to, her feminine nature. She is doing something that would scarcely be possible for a man to do, unless he were a Chinese. [Note the racism.] Could he, for instance, be a nursemaid or run a kindergarten? When I speak of injury, I do not mean merely physiological injury, but above all psychic injury. It is a woman's outstanding characteristic that she can do anything for the love of a man. But those women who can achieve something important for the love of a thing are most exceptional, because this does not agree with their nature. Love for a thing is a man's prerogative.[12]

Jung believed that women's consciousness was characterized by "Eros" — the ability to make connections. On the other hand, the consciousness of men exhibited "Logos" characteristics — a fact which made men more capable of analytic thought. "In men," Jung said, "Eros, the function of relationships, is usually less developed than Logos. In women, on the other hand, Eros is an expression of their true nature, while their Logos is often only a regrettable accident."[13] In Jung's opinion, it was the deficiency in Logos that made it impossible for a woman to work like a man.

The ineradicable Eros nature of the feminine is elaborated in Jung's anima/animus model of the psyche. Anima/animus theory postulates a contrasexual personality in each sex. In men this personality would be female (anima) — in women, male (animus). The word *personality,* however, is too light. In Jungian thought, anima and animus are weighty words conjuring up associations with the unconscious and the soul. The terms *Eros* and *Logos* are analogous to *anima* and *animus* in that both sets of words are rarely clearly defined and are often used with differing connotations. This slippery quality serves to insulate the ideas from much questioning. In Jungian usage of the terms, the only element one can be sure of is that an anima is man's picture of his female "other" side, while an animus is woman's picture of her "other" side. The model sets a psychological task of getting in contact with this "other."

Jung defines the anima and the animus as archetypes. On a practical level, this means that a woman's basic nature is dictated by Eros and that her capacity for logical thought should never be pushed too far. This is the origin of the continual Jungian warning about "women's libbers" overstepping the bounds of appropriately feminine use of the intellect. I am often termed *animus-ridden* when I speak to Jungian audiences about the logical flaws in the anima/animus theory. No matter how demurely I dress for a lecture, I am sure to be warned about departing too far from femininity as soon as I raise doubts about the universality of inferior Logos in women. To Jungians, the anima and animus are unchangeable archetypes for the sexes. Because they are *called* archetypes, they are supposed to remain fundamentally unchanged *per aeternitatem.* A bit of research into how Jung discovered this pair of universal archetypes raises serious doubts about the credibility of the theory. Jung tells us that a good deal of his thinking about the animus in women was deduced from what he observed about the anima in men. He wrote:

Since the anima is an archetype that is found in men, it is reasonable to suppose that an equivalent archetype must be present in women; for just as the man is compensated by a feminine element, so woman is compensated by a masculine one. I do not, however, wish this argument to give the impression that these compensatory relationships were arrived at by deduction. On the contrary, long and varied experience was needed in order to grasp the nature of anima and animus empirically. Whatever we have to say about these archetypes, therefore, is either directly verifiable or at least rendered probable by the facts. At the same time, I am fully aware that we are discussing pioneer work which by its very nature can only be provisional.[14]

The hesitation, the assertion of probability and the mention of "pioneer work" at the end of the paragraph reveal Jung's uncertainty about the idea. The key statement is the first sentence: *"Since the anima is an archetype that is found in men, it is reasonable to suppose that an equivalent archetype must be present in women."* Jung certainly seems to have deduced the presence of the animus in women from his hypothesis of an anima in men.

Jung never developed the animus idea to the extent of his anima theory. I suggest further development was impossible because he was forcing a mirror image where there was none. He hypothesized the animus in woman to balance the anima in men. The reasoning was that if the unconscious in men was a feminine anima, in women, it must be a masculine animus. According to the Jungian stereotypes of masculine and feminine, this gives women and men qualitatively different kinds of unconsciouses. Certainly this is a startlingly broad assertion based on so little evidence. The anima/animus model and its goal of unification works better for men than for women. The model supports stereotyped notions of what masculine and feminine are by adding mystification to guard against change in the social sphere, where women are at a huge disadvantage. In practice, men can keep control of all Logos activities and appropriate just whatever Eros they need from their women as a psychological hobby. Women, on the other hand, are not encouraged to develop Logos. Instead, they are thought of as handicapped by nature in all Logos areas — such as those found at the top of any important profession. Acceptance of the anima/animus theory does not support integration of the sexes, but rather leads to more separatism. Intrapsychically, the theory might do some good for people who have been afraid of experiences that have been seen as appropriate for just one sex or the other. To people with these fears, the anima/animus theory says, "Go ahead, develop your contrasexual element." However, the model is decidedly inadequate if a person is questioning the masculine and feminine stereotypes themselves.

Along with many other facets of Jung's theory, the imbalance of the anima/animus model was never challenged by any of his immediate circle of followers. In fact, they were and are prone to emphasize it to an even greater degree than he did. Dr. Jolande Jacobi, one of the most successful female members of the second generation of Jungians, insisted that "just as the male by his very nature is uncertain in the realm of Eros, so the woman will always be unsure in the realm of Logos."[15] The fact that Dr. Jacobi's very successful career as author and lecturer in the realm of Logos seemed to contradict this statement never bothered her at all. Jacobi was typical of many

Jungians in that she did not let the facts of any individual's experience contradict an archetype that she wanted to believe was universal.

We all enjoy the Logos act of enterprise — of using our brains and nervous systems to formulate goals and to strive to reach them. There is erotic delight in the use of the mind. When a housewife plans a dinner party, chooses her menu and considers her guests and their possible interactions, is she not engaged in a Logos activity? Likewise, when a businessman plans a meeting, determines his agenda and imagines his colleagues and the interplay betweeen them, is he not involved with a good bit of Eros? The Jungian categories of anima and animus, Logos and Eros serve as smoke screens, veiling critical thought about experience and mental processes. Their very vagueness is seductive for lazy intellects who want to rest in the security that their prejudices reflect universal truths.

The archetypes of anima, animus and their verbal handmaidens, Eros and Logos, have inspired a great deal of Jungian lore. It is the concept of archetype that allowed Jungians like Erich Neumann and Esther Harding[16] to claim universal status for their studies of the feminine psyche. Such studies rest on a careful pruning of mythological material to conform to the specifications of a predefined archetype of femininity. The archetypes of positive mother, negative mother, amazon or courtesan are asserted to be unchanging and absolute patterns of female experience. Jungians do not realize that their archetypes are descriptions of cultural conditions that are rooted in history. Instead, they prefer to see archetypes as the inescapable determinants of history.

Unfortunately, any social group or gender that is being stereotyped or, rather, archetyped by such logic is thus effectively discouraged from attempting to deviate from the preordained categories. The assumption that an attitude, an image or a behavior pattern is archetypal stops

Jungians from seeking the circumstances that cause it to arise. For example, we would not ask why relatively few women become physicists or engineers once we have assumed that an inferior Logos archetype determines the consciousness of women. Furthermore, if we believe that the deficient Logos is archetypal, we make no effort to change educational practices or hiring procedures that discourage women from attempting Logos careers. The archetype becomes the functional equivalent of "God's will," which it is quite hopeless and downright immoral to fight.

Deciding that our stereotypes are archetypes can only impede progress. The roots of sexism and racism run deep in human culture. We need to call on the methods of every academic and scientific discipline to discover the reasons for such prejudices and to formulate an effective means of combating them.

A formal critique and revision of the Jungian archetype is a task to which feminist analysis is obligated. Since it is women who have been most limited by the assumption of absolute determinants at work in human life, it is up to women to question any philosophy which tends to create absolute categories. If feminists do not redefine the archetype, we are left with only two options: The first is to accept the patriarchal ideas of feminine as ultimate and unchanging and work within those; the second is to indulge in a rival search to find our own archetypes — this time the *true* ones to support our conclusions.

Quite a few feminists are taking the second option. An example is the trend to proclaim matriarchy as historical fact and to draw conclusions about the superiority of women based on such facts. Although much research into the role of females in prehistory needs to be done[17] and although there is great psychological value in cultivating visions of female power,[18] facile assumptions about the archetypal nature of feminine superiority should be avoided, I believe. Such assertions of an empirical absolute based on shaky evidence are the very same means men have employed to justify the subjugation of women. While we must recover lost history and buried images of women, we ought not to set up these images as archetypes. If we do, we run the risk of setting bounds to experience by defining what the proper experience of women is. This could become a new version of the ideology of the Eternal Feminine and it could result in structures just as limiting as those prescribed by the old Eternal Feminine. We must redefine the archetype and experiment with new attitudes to myth and iconography. (The traditional notion of archetypes implies that they are better and grander than the dreams, fantasies and imaginal experiences that all of us have.)

The term *image* refers to any pictorial pattern that abides in our own mental structures. These pictorial images that we experience in dream, fantasy and vision are not, however, merely in the mind. On the contrary, images structure our behavior and actions in the material world as well. This is why therapies that work with the imagination are effective. When we work with images, we work with the conscious and subconscious agendas we live by. Images are thus always in dialogue with action. What we *do* in our lives is related to what we think about our lives. (Even though some people lead grand imaginal lives and plod out dull everyday existences, there is still a correlation. The very dullness of life often inspires the grandeur of the imagination.) When we change our actions, we influence our imaginal patterns. Likewise, when we experience new imaginal currents, our doings in the world and feelings about what we do tend to change also.

Archetypes, in the traditional view, are loftier than images. In Jungian thought, archetypes are believed to be the ideal and somehow transcendent patterns which the contents of our own minds (i.e., the images) can only approximate. This separation leads to making a distinction between the ideal form out there in archetype land and the expressed content in here, in individuals — in their activities, dreams and meditations.

Thinking of archetypes in this manner devalues the facts of experience. It encourages us to give close attention to experience only when it approximates an archetypal absolute. Many Christians, for example, treat Jesus's life as their only archetype. They grant most attention to the parts of their lives that can be seen as conforming to his. The parts of their lives that do not reflect Jesus's life do not receive such attention and are treated as ungodlike and mundane. Sexuality becomes highly problematic because there is so little of it in what we know of Jesus's life. Likewise, the lives of women seem inferior because they differ so enormously in both form and focus from the life of Christ.

No matter how many archetypes we recognize, as long as we think of archetypes as transcendent, distant patterns, we are bound to set limits to human thought and aspirations. The fall of the great patriarchal faiths is going to give us a chance to experiment with more democratic forms of religiosity. Perhaps we can do without the concept of archetype as a transcendent model of behavior "out there" in heaven or "back then" in history. The transcendent, perfect forms we have imagined to date have led us to treat certain races, a certain sex and certain parts of ourselves as unworthy of our best attention and energy because they do not conform to the ideal. By refusing to set up transcendent categories we might see the world with new eyes. We could stay open to the data of more of our own experience and treat the contents of our own minds with new respect and reflection.

As a step in this direction, feminist philosophy should refuse to set up either new absolutes or archetypes. We should experiment with a line of thought that begins to equate image (and, its correlate, action) with archetype. Toward the end of his life, Jung toyed with the idea of a psychoid continuum on which our action in the world, our images of that action, and the ideal archetype were linked. Although he continued to insist on the transcendence of archetypes, he was beginning to join them to the material world of experience through images.[19] We can go further than Jung and stop entertaining notions of transcendence altogether. We could begin to consider image and archetype as synonymous. Such a theoretical movement could lead us to put much greater value on what is happening in an individual's life and psyche. We would also be less inclined to insist that an image be unchanging in order to be important. In an age of rapid change in lives and perceptions, an ability to value the kaleidoscopic variety in imaginal life would be a comforting and significant talent to foster.

"Archetypal" might be usefully employed as an adjective to describe the degree to which an image affects us. Each fantasy, dream or life story could be classified by the impact it carries for our lives, our communities and the times of our history. We could begin to understand that what binds us together as human beings is not, in fact, the *contents* of our religious and psychic imagery but rather the continual *process* of producing and reflecting on imagery. It is not necessary to cling to past documents of the imaginal process to maintain religious communities. Instead, we could build communities around the observing and sharing of the imaginal process alive in all of us.

JUNG'S DISCOVERY OF THE RELIGIOUS
PROCESS WITHIN

We can return to Jung to use his insights into the interior religious process now that we have critiqued the function of archetype in his theory. (His ideas about religious innovation are expressed throughout the *Collected Works* and the published *Letters*.) A good way to approach the topic is to use material from his autobiography, *Memories, Dreams, Reflections*. It is in this account of his life and work that Jung tells us why he had to free himself from biblical creeds and how he developed a religious outlook based on visions, fantasies and dreams.

Jung says that he began to understand the importance of cultivating personal forms of religious expression at age twelve. He learned this from a vision he had about the local cathedral:

One fine summer day . . . I came out of school at noon and went to the cathedral square. The sky was gloriously blue, the day one of radiant sunshine. The roof of the cathedral glittered, the sun sparkling from the new, brightly glazed tiles. I was overwhelmed by the beauty of the sight, and thought: "The world is beautiful and the church is beautiful and God made all this and sits above it far away in the blue sky on a golden throne and . . ."[20]

Then Jung tried to stop himself from thinking. He had a great sense of foreboding and experienced "a choking sensation." "I felt numbed," he writes, "and knew only: Don't go on thinking now! Something terrible is coming, something I do not want to think, something I dare not even approach. Why not? Because I would be committing the most frightful of sins."[21] Jung tells us that he fought against his vision for days. Eventually he gave up and allowed the thought to come:

I gathered all my courage, as though I were about to leap forthwith into hell-fire, and let the thought come. I saw before me the cathedral, the blue sky. God sits on His golden throne, high above the world — and from under the throne an enormous turd falls upon the sparkling new roof, shatters it, and breaks the walls of the cathedral asunder.[22]

Jung's description of his feelings right *after* this vision contains his most revealing statements about God, tradition, the Bible and Church. His comments deserve careful attention:

I felt an enormous, an indescribable relief. Instead of the expected damnation, grace had come upon me, and with it an unutterable bliss such as I had never known. I wept for happiness and gratitude. The wisdom and goodness of God had been revealed to me now that I had yielded to His inexorable command. It was as though I had experienced an illumination. A great many things I had not previously understood became clear to me. That was what my father had not understood, I thought; he had failed to experience the will of God, had opposed it for the best reasons and out of the deepest faith. And that was why he had never experienced the miracle of grace which heals all and makes all comprehensible.[23]

Jung goes on to tell us that his father did not understand the independent outlook that his own vision of living religion had taught him:

He had taken the Bible's commandments as his guide; he believed in God as the Bible prescribed and as his forefathers had taught him. But he did not know the immediate living God who stands, omnipotent and free, above His Bible and His Church, who calls upon man to partake of his freedom, and can force him to renounce his own views and convictions in order to fulfill without reserve the command of God. In His trial of human courage God refuses to abide by traditions, no matter how sacred.[24]

From this contrast with his father's views, we can see that from the age of twelve, Jung had already decided that institutional religious dogma and the Bible were secondary to the "immediate living God." Because this decision had been made on the basis of a fantasy vision, we can understand why Jung valued imaginal activity so highly. His lifelong stance against the religious creeds that stifled fantasy activity in individuals becomes clearer in light of the important information that fantasy activity had provided him in his early youth.

In the light of the background of Jung's attitude to any creed or dogma that prescribed the forms religious experience should take, I do not think *revelation* is too strong a term to describe the goal of Jung's interest in dream and fantasy. For him they were a genuine source of religious insight. He always encouraged his patients to do what he had done by letting their internal imaginal processes provide their own religious direction.[25] The revelation Jung encouraged in his patients gave them access to the spiritual processes at work in their own psyches, independent of the religiosity endorsed by traditional religions. When Jung tells us that most of his cures worked by restoring a religious outlook to a patient, he is referring to religion as an activity of reflection on interior imagery.

Jung's prime method for acquainting patients with their own imagery lay in urging them to take dream activity very seriously. He developed instructions for dreaming the dream onward though the method of active imagination. This process could be used on any product of mental activity. The goal was to go where the dream or fantasy was leading:

Take the unconscious in one of its handiest forms, say a spontaneous fantasy, a dream, an irrational mood, an affect, or something of the kind, and operate with it. Give it your special attention, concentrate on it, and observe its alterations objectively. Spare no effort to devote yourself to this task, follow the subsequent transformations of the spontaneous fantasy attentively and carefully. Above all, don't let anything from outside, that does not belong, get into it, for the fantasy image has "everything it needs."[26]

Jung believed that a person was engaged in spiritual activity when she or he followed the transformations of dream or fantasy. Curiously, though this is a dominant theme of Jung's work, he was slow to state it explicitly. His first move toward ascribing a religious function to the dream was evident in 1914 with his paper entitled "On Psychological Understanding."[27] In this paper, he distinguished two modes of psychological understanding. One derives from the "causal standpoint," which seeks to trace a symptom back to its original cause. The other, which he holds in higher esteem, derives from what Jung called the "constructive standpoint." The constructive standpoint led one to understand the goal to which the symptom was leading:

> Just as through analysis and reduction of individual events the causal method ultimately arrives at the universal principles of human psychology, so through the synthesis of individual trends the constructive method aims at universal goals. The psyche is the point of intersection, hence it must be defined under two aspects. On the one hand it gives a picture of the remnants and traces of all that has been, and, on the other, but expressed in the same picture, the outlines of what is to come, in so far as the psyche creates its own future.[28]

Jung thus established a purposeful function for the analysis of dreams by suggesting that dream imagery be studied from his constructive standpoint. Such a method, he believed, would yield insights into the future psychic outlook of the dreamer.

Jung did not explicitly connect the constructive standpoint with a religious attitude toward the dream until 1933 in his essay entitled "The Meaning of Psychology for Modern Man."[29] In this essay, Jung spoke directly of the use of dreams to provide spiritual insight. He writes about the spiritual problem he saw arising in the modern age — of the failure of contemporary religions to provide many people with a religious outlook that would give them a sense of meaning. Jung suggests that a solution could be found in dreams. Expecting people to be displeased with this answer, he said, "I admit that I fully understand the disappointment of my patient and of my public when I point to dreams as a source of information in the spiritual confusion of our modern world."[30] In the essay he describes the dream as a religious entity in rather halting and apologetic tones. He alludes to other "things besides dreams," which he "can not discuss":

> If I spoke before chiefly of dreams, I did so because I wished to draw attention to one of the most immediate approaches to the

world of inner experience. But there are many things besides dreams which I cannot discuss here. The investigation of the deeper levels of the psyche brings to light much that we, on the surface, can at most dream about. No wonder, then, that sometimes the strongest and most original of all man's spiritual activities — the religious activity — is also discovered from our dreams.[31]

Though "The Meaning of Psychology for Modern Man" is written in a rather diffident tone, it contains some of Jung's strongest statements about the connection of dreams to religious activity. Jung was always aware of how sensitive theologians were to such suggestions. Three months before his death in June 1961, Jung wrote a grateful letter to the Reverend John A. Sanford thanking the clergyman for sending him a sermon he had delivered in Los Angeles on the importance of dreams. From the letter, we can see how careful Jung felt he had to be when mentioning the subject of dreams in a theological context:

Dear Mr. Sanford,

Thank you very much for kindly sending me your sermon on the importance of dreams. I have read it with interest and pleasure. It is a historical event, as you are — so far as my knowledge goes — the first one who has called the attention of the Christian congregation to the fact that the Voice of God can still be heard if you are only humble enough. . . .

The understanding of dreams should indeed be taken seriously by the Church, since the *cura animarum* is one of its duties, which has been sadly neglected by the Protestants. Even if confession is a relatively poor version of the *cura*, the Catholic Church knows at least the function of the *directeur de conscience*, a highly important function which is unknown to the Protestants.

I admire your courage and sincerely hope that you will not become too unpopular for mentioning a topic so heartily hated and despised by most of the theologians. This is so at least over here. There are only single individuals who risk the fight for survival. The pilgrim's way is spiked with thorns everywhere, even if he is a good Christian, or just therefore.[32]

My best wishes!

Yours sincerely,

C. G. Jung

This letter to Sanford shows how sensitive Jung was to the pitfall of offending theologians with suggestions that dreams ought to be taken seriously by religious practitioners. In fact, from the corpus of Jung's works, we can see that he viewed dreams as the "Voice of God" he mentions in his letter to Sanford. Jung considered dreams a means of attuning a patient to her or his own religious processes. But in his view, such processes should not be codified by religious institutions. Jung wanted religion to be a phenomenon that always remained open to each individual's conception of it as that conception was revealed in the activities of dream and fantasy.

Although Jung deserves sharp criticism for those areas of his work that fell short of his ideals of respect and dignity for individual psychic values, he ought not to be dismissed on account of his worst work.

Jung's analysis of the religious nature of fantasy and dream is of crucial importance for anyone interested in providing alternatives to religious activity as prescribed by traditional institutions. As a feminist, I must harshly criticize Jung and his followers for their prejudices about women, "primitives" and the "feminine." Nevertheless, I am intrigued with Jung's use of fantasies and dreams as streams of imagery that can inspire religious reflection. The Jungian method may point to a source of religious iconography accessible to everyone, a source particularly appealing to those of us who are not entirely at home with orthodox creeds.

I like to think that Jung would have approved of subjecting his ideas to criticism so that his best wisdom might be employed by future generations. "I can only hope and wish," Jung once wrote, "that no one becomes 'Jungian.' I stand for no doctrine, but describe facts and put forward certain views which I hold worthy of discussion. . . . I proclaim no cut-and-dried doctrine and I abhor 'blind adherents.' I leave everyone free to deal with the facts in his own way, since I also claim this freedom for myself."[33] In the coming time of religious change, the "Great Men" can be no more sacrosanct than can be the "Great Gods." We must pick and choose among the theories of the ages. Our constructions need to be various and flexible in order to let human nature attempt to define itself in new terms.

In the next chapters, I will explore some of the new methods, theories, images and religions that have sprouted up in these early times of the Changing of the Gods. The forms I have chosen are those most likely to further living religion — initially for women, whose present need is greatest, but gradually for men too. Whenever I see the new beginnings running the risk of becoming new creeds, I will try to be as critical of them as I have been of Jung.

I am aware that by holding to ideals of flux and change for the new religious patterns, I may be accused of advocating a creed. Such is the universal paradox in any attempt at a theory that strives for pluralism and non-universality. If we must indeed have some creeds in an age of new gods and new possibilities, I hope that they will be written on water and open to life.

Chapter 6

AND FROM HIS CORPSE THERE FIRST AROSE LILITH, MARY, THE SISTERHOOD AND ANDROGYNES TO TAKE HIS PLACE

WHEN a symbol as pervasive as that of the father-god begins to die, tremendous anxiety is generated. Other images arise to take its place almost immediately. Candidates for different god images are already being nominated either to replace the father-god or to provide him with a female retinue. A survey of these new images shows that some are more conducive to freedom of thought than others.

REBELS OF THE BIBLE

Jewish legend tells us that Eve was not Adam's first wife. Immediately after the creation of Adam, God made a woman to keep him company. Her name was Lilith.

Adam and Lilith quarreled at once. She refused to lie below him while making love. He refused to lie below her as well. "I will not lie below you," he said, "for you are fit to be below me and I above you."

"We are both equal because we both come from the earth," Lilith insisted.

The argument continued. Lilith uttered the "Ineffable Name of God" and flew away.

God sent three angels after Lilith with this message: If she did not go back to Adam, one hundred of her children would die each day. Even so, Lilith refused to return.[1] Throughout the centuries, rabbis have hated Lilith. They made her into a monster who visited men at night and caused wet dreams and sterility. They spoke of her as a mother of demons who killed women in childbirth and destroyed newborn babies. Lilith, the first woman who attempted liberation, has received terrible press in the Jewish religious media.

Times are changing. In 1972, Judith Plaskow extended the Lilith story. She imagined Eve climbing the walls of Eden every night to talk with Lilith.

> They sat and spoke together, of the past and then of the future. They talked not once, but many times and for many hours. They taught each other many things, and told each other stories, and laughed together, and cried, over and over, till the bond of sisterhood grew between them. . . . And God and Adam were expectant and afraid the day Eve and Lilith returned to the garden, bursting with possibilities, ready to rebuild it together.[2]

Plaskow is creating a new image for Lilith, an image derived from Lilith's original biblical role of defiance to Adam but amplified by bringing her back from banishment to construct a new order. The new story of Lilith opens up channels for different visions of new religious patterns to be created while maintaining touch with the Judaeo-Christian symbol system. Lilith has inspired several Jewish women to found a feminist magazine in her honor. *Lilith* magazine is published quarterly as a forum for women to examine and criticize Jewish patriarchal tradition.[3] The editors see Lilith as Adam's equal, "the embodiment of independent womanhood."

Another female biblical rebel who is being revisioned in feminist terms is Queen Vashti, the first wife of Ahasuarus. In the Book of Esther we read that the king held a feast for the princes of the land as a means of exhibiting his wealth and power. As the evening went on and the drinking increased, the princes began to brag about their beautiful women. Ahasuarus called his wife, Vashti, to appear at the party and display her great beauty. Vashti refused. The king was furious. He divorced Vashti and cut her off from all royal wealth. When he remarried, he chose Esther, the beautiful (and subservient!) cousin of Mordecai.

Jewish feminist Mary Gendler has traced the figure of Vashti in rabbinic legend. Gendler found that the rabbis vilified Vashti because of her disobedience to a man just as they had vilified Lilith for defying Adam. Male Jewish scholars visualized Vashti with leprosy and turned her into an aggressive enemy of the Jewish people. All this simply because Vashti refused to display herself before the king![4]

Gendler suggests that instead of all Jewish girls dressing up as the obedient Esther at Purim, some Jewish girls should dress up as the rebellious Vashti. Thus, another biblical image of a proud, assertive woman could begin to be redeemed.

It is clear, however, that new honors for Lilith and Vashti cannot save Judaism or the Old Testament for Jewish women. These rebels are minor characters in a drama in which men have the best parts. Nevertheless, reimagining the rebels is a good beginning for religious revolution. The Vashtis and Liliths of biblical tradition give us mythic predecessors who dared to oppose the ancient patriarchs. They can serve as muses for the work of opposing the patriarchs of modern times.

We must re-evaluate all female images that have been despised by previous generations of male scholars. Behind every witch, dragoness and temptress there is a vision of female power — power that society is now ready to understand and, perhaps, to embrace. In comparison with the rebels, the good girls of biblical tradition have little to offer.

THE VIRGIN MARY — THE GOOD GIRL
OF CHRISTIANITY

Some years ago, while walking along the lakeshore in Zurich, I saw a defaced statue of the Virgin Mary. Someone had painted genitals on the Virgin! I was intrigued. Whoever did the artwork probably did not realize the political statement he or she was making. Mary has certainly been desexed in Christian tradition. The painter was restoring her sexuality.

Obsession with purifying Mary of any taint of womanhood has occupied Christian scholars for centuries. Treatises on the Holy Mother's hymen abound in every Catholic research library. Theologians have insisted that Mary remained "intact" before, during (!) and after the birth of Jesus. Traditions also speak of how Mary's body never decayed and never gave off odors. Instead, her physical body remained perfect even after death.

Mary is certainly the good girl of Christianity. Absolutely obedient to the male God, she derives all her status from her son. Because of her absolute purity and obedience, she is the only pinup girl who has been permitted in monks' cells throughout the ages.

However, Mary has a legitimate base of power in the human psyche. Behind her sanitized figure lurk all the great pagan goddesses of the ancient world. Like Persephone, goddess of the underworld, Mary intercedes on behalf of the dead. Like the earth goddesses Cybele, Gaia and Demeter, Mary is prior to God and forms the ground of His being. Like the virgins — Athena and Artemis — Mary is free from bonds of marriage to mortal men. Mary derives her power in the fact that she compels minds and hearts from the vestiges of these vibrant goddesses she was supposed to replace.[5]

Mary has been castrated by popes, cardinals, priests and theologians, by all who fear the sexual and emotional power of natural womanhood. We must be suspicious of all modern efforts to tout Mary as the "liberated woman of Christianity" as Pope Paul suggested in 1974. In fact, the Church will never allow Mary to be a deity equal to Jesus. Neither will she be permitted to be a mortal woman capable of independent thought and action. It would be far better for women to contemplate the images of the great goddesses behind the myth of Mary than to dwell on the man-made image of Mary herself.

There is another danger in using any aspect of Mary's image as a model for modern women. Since Mary is the perfect woman of Christianity, she tends to be proposed as the only possible model for all women — the model we all should aspire to become. This regiments our imagination around a single stereotype. For example, in her essay "Daring to Grow," Pat Driscoll suggests that Mary in her pregnancy be adopted as a "valid role model for all." Driscoll, mother of eleven, says that for twenty years she had been "developing a fresh focus on Mary, Mother of Jesus, as woman-with-child, our universal mother and symbol of ecumenical unity and feminist solidarity."[6] She insists that the pregnant Mary is "the New Woman we all dream of becoming: caring, joyful, free, creative and totally fulfilled."[7]

The cheerful autocracy in suggesting this image of Mary as a role model for everyone should not go unnoticed. An image that works for one woman is assumed to work for every woman. Driscoll imitates the same methodology that feminists since Stanton's day have revealed as the practice of male theologians. Like the Church Fathers, she has proclaimed that something that works for her is universally true.

Driscoll's recognition of an image that provides religious reflection for her joy in pregnancy is both admirable and valid — admirable because she has been able to articulate the phenomenon, and valid because the image arises from twenty years of her experience. It is invalid, however, to claim that her pregnant Mary is "the New Woman we all dream of becoming," since testimony abounds to show that many women dream of no such thing. By setting up a new idol, Driscoll denies the process by which she reached her own illumination — the process of twenty years of becoming attuned to a vision that enlivened her. No one told Pat Driscoll to worship the pregnant Mary because she was universally true and proper to all. How then can she presume to impart this to other women as gospel truth? If Driscoll is to remain true to her path toward her image, she has to allow others the same option, even if this means disclosure of other paths and other images, which may directly contradict and thus threaten her pregnant Mary.

It is possible for one image to threaten another only if the authenticity of the one originally put forward is based on an assertion of universality. If Driscoll were to see her Mary as authentic but, nevertheless, contingent to her particular psychic situation, even a vision such as a child-slaughtering Medea would in no way invalidate her relation to the Holy Mother. It is only when an image is asserted to hold a monotheistic and universal posture that it is vulnerable to attack by relativism — by facing the power that other images can hold for other individuals with other psychic patterns.

One image or one feminine principle can exist only if all females agree about the significance of the chosen symbol or if all those who do not agree are considered deficient in regard to their femininity. I maintain that the consequence of searching for a single image only duplicates the exclusivism that feminists have shown to be the root of patriarchal practices. No single image of woman can reflect all the important values of all females. The desire of some feminists to endorse any one image of proper femininity could be a desire to stereotype women into a new role and to limit their possibilities. Instead of contracting our vision around one goal and one image, we ought to be exploring the broadest implications of feminist theory, i.e., the elimination of gender stereotypes altogether.

Gender stereotypes will be eliminated when we recognize that women and men can have many different styles of thought, feeling and behavior. One person can live many myths in a single lifetime or, in some cases, in a single year. In this age of change for our gods we need to proliferate the ways we allow ourselves to imagine psychological and religious styles. Let us not endorse *one* goddess or *one* image as embodying the ideals of the new age. Why not see the different people we all might become by looking at many myths and images?

THE ANDROGYNE

An image with utopian overtones that is being considered as a substitute for the fallen patriarchal god is the androgyne. This is a tricky image which needs to be considered very carefully.

The androgyne is often invoked by people who want to deny the problems and anguish women in this society must face. I saw a classic example of this two years ago at a nationwide conference on Jungian psychology. A well-known woman who has written about androgyny was introduced by a younger woman student. The student told the audience how happy she was to welcome such a great woman to her campus. When the psychologist took the microphone, she admonished the student for referring to her as a woman, since she felt she was "beyond that now." During my presentation I remarked that the psychologist still looked like a woman to me. If she had been a man and were introduced as a man, I said, I did not think she would have been prompted to tell us she was beyond her sexual identity. In many intellectual circles at present, men can succeed and androgynes can succeed — but women still cannot. Concern for androgyny is a stance some people adopt to avoid being labeled a shrill women's libber who insists on respect for real women.

In feminist religious writings, a proclamation of androgyny is often used to end an essay on a theatrical (if not truly operatic) cadence. One feminist scholar, for example, concludes an essay on women and religion by resolving that "both men and women must be free to live androgynously in everyday life and in response to the ultimate dimensions of life in ways that combine and transcend specific masculinity and femininity."[8] I find such recommendations hollow and unreal.

The tendency to hail the androgyne in an otherworldly call to a new world order is a very ancient Christian use of the symbol. In "The Image of the Androgyne: Some Uses of a Symbol in Earliest Christianity," Wayne A. Meeks shows how the androgyne was used as a popular symbol of salvation in late Hellenism.[9] Meeks explains that the early Christians adapted the androgyne to the sacrament of baptism to symbolize the new world to come. "If in baptism the Christian has put on again the image of the Creator, in whom 'there is no male and female,' then for him the old world has passed away and, behold! the new has come."[10] Thus, the androgyne was not meant as a Christian symbol of this world, but always of the next. Although history has shown that the image of an *androgynous* creator-god proved unworkable and a male god dominated Christian minds for two millennia, Meeks is hopeful that the symbol might still triumph. In the early Church, the androgyne "proved too dangerously ambivalent" to be viable and "the declaration that in Christ there is no more male and female faded into innocuous metaphor." Nevertheless, Meeks surmises that the androgyne may yet find its "proper moment" to emerge.[11] I doubt that the androgyne will ever emerge. Instead, it will perpetually tempt us with vagueness. Seeing androgyny as the be-all to end-all can only keep sexual equality dangerously ambivalent and out of the mainstream of psychic life. In imaginal history, androgynes always have a way of appearing at the end of things. Ovid, for example, envisioned his androgyne as a dead creature resulting from the drowning of a man and woman entangled together at the bottom of a riverbed. In the symbolism of Tarot cards, the androgynous figure appears as the last card of the major arcana and represents a vague and ephemeral vision occurring at the end of the symbolic cycle.

In current religious philosophy, the androgyny motif from St. Paul is functioning with the same seductive haziness as the androgyne in Ovid and on Tarot cards. Mary Daly raises this issue when she asks "What sense does it make to assert that in *Christ* 'there is neither male nor female'? Wasn't 'Christ' an exclusively male symbol, even though somewhat 'feminized'? What on earth, then, could the text mean? But that is the point: it could not mean anything *on earth,* where there definitely were and are females and males."[12] Meeks's research suggests that St. Paul never intended the statement to refer to any state of grace on earth, but rather to the salvation to come. From all of St. Paul's other statements about women, we know he preferred males to reign over females on earth.

I have noticed that even when the symbol of the androgyne is detached from Christ as it is in much contemporary androgyny theorizing, the figure still retains an unrealistic, otherworldly quality. It is this quality that makes the symbol a risky one for feminists probing their present experience to find theological roots. Androgyny distracts from concentration on present experience if we continue to see it as *the* one goal or god to be reached. However, if androgyny can be considered as only *one* image of future time within the present, it need not be encountered as a megalith that blocks access to other images. Instead, it can be enjoyed for the surreal, dreamy state it inspires.

Despite its rather disappointing history as an image of practical salvation, there is one understanding of androgyny that can foster realistic reflection on the two sexes of this world. This is possible if the concept is understood dynamically as meaning a plurality of sexual styles. This is the sense in which Carolyn Heilbrun uses the term in *Toward a Recognition of Androgyny*.[13] Heilbrun never really defines androgyny at all: instead, she uses it as a tool to examine novels, plays and communities in which men and women shifted from what were considered proper sexual norms. Heilbrun employs the word *androgyny* to inspire the "imagination of possibilities" once human beings can begin a "release from the prison of gender."[14] Understood in this way, androgyny can be used as a stimulus for the imagination. Rita Gross has made the practical suggestion that cross-cultural anthropological study of religious phenomena be based on interviews with both male and female members of the religious community at the outset. (At present most studies are based on data collected only from men.) An androgynous method of data collection in anthropology would insure that both male and female experience would be studied.

Androgyny is not an image at all. Instead, it is a concept that can engender a panoply of images. If we perceive androgyny as a beginning, it calls for an imaginative philosophy that allows for plurality. However, as an endpoint, androgyny appears insubstantial — veiled in heavenly fluff — a rather impotent label for two sexes alive in this world.

A FATHER-GOD WHO KNOWS HIS PLACE

Whatever images do live in the new order of gods, a father-god is sure to be among them. As we develop our psycho-religious awareness to allow all that we are to surface in the form of images, we must expect father-gods to appear in one way or another. These gods will remain part of us even though the size, shape, color and location of that part will change. Although father-gods will no longer stand in the center of our culture, they will continue to walk through it.

I do not expect that the continued presence of male gods will be harmful to women. Women experience psychic oppression only when father-gods are touted as the sole images of the highest religious value in a society. This condition defines patriarchy, fosters scorn for women and dupes women into believing that they are innately inferior to men. However, when father-gods are present within a panoply of psycho-religious images, they can no longer enforce their former tyranny. Women will be free to reconsider Christ and Yahweh and to find new places for them.

At the present time, there are many reasons for a woman who is freeing herself from patriarchy to hang on to the father in some part of her soul. Women who are making up their own lives — who are cutting out new patterns — must use large swatches of material from their past. I have one close friend for whom the father-god is still very important even though she is now a worshiper of the Goddess in the Sisterhood of the Wicca. My friend readily admits that she still needs the father. "I can't get angry at the Goddess," she told me. "I need the Goddess to love and pray to. But I need a male god to scream at for making life so sad. I know this is a primitive way to think — to make the Goddess all good and the male god all bad. But this is how I feel."

Not all followers of the goddess need to maintain such dualism. As we will see in the next chapter, many modern witches do not make distinctions between positive and negative forces in their conceptions of the Goddess. To many witches, She who represents life and nurture is also involved with death and decay. For my friend, however, the Goddess had only good, pleasant, life-giving qualities. Everything bad was relegated to a male god. My friend needs the father to embody all that is wrong with the world. She is not alone. In contemporary feminist culture and in the next few years ahead, the father will live in the hatred of women who need a god to blame. Putting a single deity in charge of evil is actually a Christian tendency. Specific Christian images of the good Christ and the evil Satan will fade long before general Christian styles of imagining die out. The theological habit of dividing the world into two warring camps will be reflected in the imagination of many feminists as they grow out of Christianity. While they are growing, many women will keep the father-god alive in their need for a psychic figure to represent negative feelings.

As feminists mellow, it will become less crucial to blame the father for all that is wrong with the world. We will be able to imagine our gods in a less simplistic fashion. Many images will have their dark spots — their negative qualities — and fathers eventually will not have to be painted entirely black.

When we have stopped hating the father, we will find that he lives in other ways. We can expect him to seduce us from time to time. Many of us will be drawn to speculating about the life of Jesus, to reading the history of the Jewish people, or to studying the mystical traditions of these religions. We must be free (and strong) enough to allow this interest to live within us.

In the new age of changes for our gods, Christ and Yahweh will no longer behave as egotistical, spoiled children in our psyches — they will no longer keep us from giving our attention to other members of our psychic families. Instead, Christ and Yahweh will be valuable images that maintain our ties with history. They will remind us of the patriarchal monotheism which we have outgrown but which we will need to remember. We should expect to treat the old gods as we treat the places of our childhood — as important places of our past which demand regular visits and recollection but where we can never live again.

There is an image emerging that many women can live with. I refer to the Goddess of feminist witchcraft. She is not vague, not perfect and not single-natured. She needs a whole chapter to herself.

Chapter 7

FEMINIST WITCHCRAFT —
THE GODDESS IS ALIVE!

Mama!
From my heart,
From my blood, Mama
I call you. . . .

My heart of your heat
Limb of your Northwind
Water of your Water
Cunt of your Hillside
Cock of your Springtime
Eyes of your stars,
    Mama
Eyes of your sun,
    Mama
Of your Sol, Mama
My soul of your Sol,
    Mama
Come Mama!
Come into our circle
Our womb
Be with us now, Mama
Be with us now!

Invocation to the Goddess as Mother
Winter Solstice 1977
by Susan Stern

Imagine: It is December 21, 1977, the Winter Solstice. Starhawk and her coven are meeting to celebrate the birthday of the sun. There is a fire in the fireplace of the large, high-ceilinged room. Two long snakeskins, recently shed by Starhawk's two pet boa constrictors, are draped from the chandelier. The twenty celebrants stand in a circle. All are nude. The women outnumber the men.

Starhawk turns to the outside of the circle, faces east, raises a wooden-handled knife and begins to summon the spirits:

> Hail, Guardians of the Watchtowers of the East,
> Powers of air —
> We invoke you and call you,
> Great golden eagle of the dawn
> Star-seeker!
> Whirlwind!
> Rising sun!
> Come to us!
> By the air that is Her breath
> Send forth your spirit
> Be here now![1]

She then traces a five-pointed star in the air.

She walks around the circle, pausing at the south, the west, and the north to invoke the powers of all points of the compass. When she returns to where she began, she announces that the circle is cast.

The women and men now sit cross-legged on the floor and Starhawk begins her invocation to the Goddess:

> Queen of the night
> Queen of the moon
> Queen of the stars
> Queen of the horns
> Queen of the earth
> Bring to us the child of light.
>
> Night sky rider
> Silver shining one
> Lady of wild things

Silver wheel
North star
Circle
Crescent
Moon-bright
Singer
Changer!
Touch us!

See with our eyes
Hear with our ears,
Breathe with our nostrils,
Kiss with our lips,
Touch with our hands,
Be here now!

The chant is a long one. Some of the other women take
turns reciting their own poems — their own invocations to
the Goddess.

"She is with us," Starhawk announces.

One of the men beats a drum to invoke the Horned God.
This chant is much less elaborate.

Seed Sower Grain Reborn
Horned God Come!
Seed Sower Grain Reborn
Horned God Come!

The drumming is a simple, but powerful three-beat thump.

"He is here," declares Starhawk, and the drumming
stops.

She turns to a man on her left and kisses him lightly on
the lips. "Thou art God," she says. "Thou art Goddess,"
he replies. He turns and passes the kiss to the woman next
to him. "Thou art Goddess," he tells her. The kiss is
passed around the circle amid smiles and some giggles.
The first phase of their ritual is complete.

What sort of religion is this? And how can we understand
its meaning? If we ask the modern, male academic world

we can expect two sorts of replies from two sorts of people. One type of scholar will laugh it off. "This ritual means nothing," he might say. "It is a parlor game for aging hippies. I won't waste any time thinking about it." Such a scholar would then probably return to his desk and write yet another article on the history of Christianity in the Reformation.

Another sort of scholar will be very solemn. "This sort of ritual is disturbing," he might say. "It is a self-conscious revival of pagan rites. This is the very thing that preceded Nazism in Germany." He would then want to hear no more about Starhawk and her coven and would proceed to prepare his next lecture on the dangers of occultism in modern America. We ought to expect such reactions from the traditional academic establishment.

The feminist scholar, however, should be more interested. She might notice that Starhawk is a female spiritual leader whose authority is accepted by both women and men. Such a scholar might speculate on whether the prominence of a female divinity has any relation to Starhawk's high position in the group. The expression of sexuality in the ritual might then become interesting to her. Even though the ritual is highly charged with sexual energy by the nudity of the coven members and by the lyrics of their chants, there is no hint of mockery or debasement of women. Fat women and old women seem as comfortable worshiping in the nude as do the thinner and younger women. There is an acceptance and honor of woman which should interest a feminist researcher to a high degree.

Perhaps the fact that many of the women have written their own chants to invoke the Goddess might also capture a feminist's attention. It seems as if this Goddess is functioning like a muse — inspiring the female members of the coven to creative work.

And, possibly, a feminist scholar might notice that in

all of these chants, the Goddess is acknowledged as an *internal* presence in the women who are worshiping her: "From my heart,/From my blood, Mama/I call you. . . ./ My heart of your heat/. . . My soul of your Sol, Mama." The fact that the worshipers name each other Goddess and God should seem significant vis à vis the intimate words of the chants, words which speak of a close bond — even an identity — between the Goddess and self. A feminist researcher might conclude that Starhawk's coven has quite a sophisticated psychological understanding of religion.

My own respect for feminist witchcraft has grown over a two-year period of association with contemporary witches. I have come to understand that modern witches are using religion and ritual as psychological tools to build individual strengths. They practice a religion that places divinity or supernatural power within the person. In a very practical sense they have turned religion into psychology.

Witchcraft is the first modern theistic religion to conceive of its deity mainly as an internal set of images and attitudes. Although witches do often speak of the times of the matriarchies, most are more concerned with that concept as a psychological and poetic force than as an historical verity. A popular aphorism among modern witches is Monique Wittig's idea put forth in *Les Guérillères:* "There was a time when you were not a slave, remember. . . . Or, failing that, invent." Witches consider any thought or fantasy real to the degree that it influences actions in the present. In this sense a remembered fact and an invented fantasy have identical psychological value. The matriarchies, i.e., the times when no woman was a slave of any man, create visions of the pride and power women are working to have in their present lives. Thus matriarchies are functioning in modern covens and in modern witches' dreams whether or not societies ruled by females ever existed in past history.

Of course, it is impossible to give definitive proof about the practices and beliefs of witches who lived many years prior to the twentieth century. It is even impossible to decide whether or not the millions of so-called witches who were brutally massacred in the Middle Ages at the urging of Christian clergymen were witches at all. Perhaps those burnings and hangings should be remembered chiefly as the most literal expression of the misogyny which smolders within the Christian tradition. Such misogyny was chiefly directed toward women who were labeled witches by the Medieval Church. No one can know whether the women who were executed actually practiced any witchcraft at all, or, if they did, whether their craft was similar to the type that feminists are engaged in today.

Scholarly arguments about the history of witchcraft have obscured serious study of the modern phenomenon. Whatever one decides about witches of the past, it is the witches of the present who are building a powerful religion. It is the theories and practices of these witches that ought to concern scholars of modern religious movements — especially scholars interested in religions with a psychological world view.

Witches, like psychologists, understand that religions impose psychological interpretations on reality. These interpretations are conveyed through the images that religions sell to their worshipers. Witches believe that by selling women a male god, Judaism and Christianity have denied women the experience of seeing themselves as divine beings. Further, women are led to perceive it right and natural that men should rule their earth the way God rules His heaven. For these reasons, witches see religious and secular change as intimately linked. When enough women no longer agree that if "God's in His heaven — all's right with the world," feminist ideals of social justice can be implemented. One high priestess has even prophesized that until vast numbers of women control their own inner space by seeing themselves as divine and rejecting the notion of a male god, they will never succeed in getting the Equal Rights Amendment declared as law. This reasoning does not seem so far-fetched when one reads the transcripts of ERA debates and sees how often God and His teachings are used to justify woman's subordinate place.

Witches want to change the internal picture that Jewish and Christian women have of a male god in heaven so that these women will no longer accept rule by males on earth. Witches also want to strengthen secular feminists by providing imaginal depth for conceptual arguments. Since witches believe that thoughts and actions form around psychological imagery, they feel that a woman will be a more effective feminist if her deep imaginal life has a feminist tone as well as her everyday political life. Like psychologists, witches practice a craft, the aim of which is to put people on better terms with their own mental life so that they can lead fuller, more productive lives. A major difference between witches and psychotherapists is that witches see the mental health of women as having important political consequences.

Although every modern coven does not call itself a feminist coven, all covens support feminist ideology to some degree. Even groups that grant men high positions and worship the Horned God on equal terms with the Goddess still permit women members more social power than has ever been available to them in Judaeo-Christian hierarchies. The prominence of a female divinity in all forms of witchcraft fosters psychological strength in all female witches.

To understand the psychological ideals of modern witchcraft one must develop a feeling for the meaning of the Goddess in contemporary witch culture. It is She who is the muse inspiring every feminist witch and high priestess at work today. She is the focus for all the mental attitudes and abilities that the Craft works to help women develop.

"MAGIC IS AFOOT"

On the evening of April 23, 1976, several hundred women came together to participate in the first national all-woman conference on women's spirituality. The keynote speeches and opening rituals were held in a church in the heart of Boston. After listening attentively to two addresses on the theme of "Womanpower: Energy Re-Sourcement," the audience became very active. In tones ranging from whispers to shouts, they chanted, "The Goddess Is Alive — Magic Is Afoot." The women evoked the Goddess with dancing, stamping, clapping and yelling. They stood on pews and danced bare-breasted on the pulpit and amid the hymnbooks. Had any sedate, white-haired clergyman been present, I am sure he would have felt the Apocalypse had arrived.

This episode during the Boston conference cannot be described as joyful. Women felt angry and bitter in a church that represented the worship of a male god. It did not matter that this particular denomination had a more liberal outlook than most. In fact, the women were angry at all religions of the fathers and took this opportunity to mock and defy those religions in a church they had rented for the occasion. The anger was not pretty but it certainly was justified. Why not be enraged with the whole Judaeo-Christian tradition for centuries of degradation of the bodies and images of women? Why not display your breasts in a place that has tried to teach you that they are things to be ashamed of, features that make you unlike God or His son? Proclaiming that the "Goddess Is Alive" in a traditional church setting is proclaiming that woman is alive, that being female is divine. The women in Boston were raising up their images as fleshly female beings to defy their culture's image of God as an immaterial male spirit. At this opening of the Boston conference the Goddess represented fierce pride in female physical presence and fury at the abuse that presence has taken from male religious authorities. The Goddess was never symbolized as an idol or a picture in this or any other ritual. Instead, She was seen as the force which had motivated each woman to be present at the first national gathering in Her honor. The Goddess experience took several forms throughout that three-day conference. Some women led workshops on music, dance and painting. They believed that any medium that permitted a woman to express her feelings and convey them to other women was an appropriate vehicle for religious sentiments. Each workshop could be considered a temporary community of Goddess worshipers. Worship consisted of sharing skills useful in the representation of spiritual life. Each woman was her own judge of what constituted spiritual experience.

The individualism allowed in the Goddess workshops is impossible in hierarchical religions like Christianity or Judaism. In these religions only sacred texts or appointed officials are allowed to determine what is religious experience and what is not. In feminist witchcraft, however, since each woman is considered a Goddess, all of her creations are in a sense holy. No one has the right to put another person's feelings into categories of sacred or profane, religious or secular. Thus, not only are the inner dynamics of a woman's psyche seen as religious processes, but she is perceived as capable of evaluating these processes herself. Each is the priestess of her own religion. Celebrant and shaman are identical.

Even the high priestesses of the feminist witchcraft movement emphasize that all women are priestesses and Goddesses. Every woman is encouraged to keep a small altar in her home to be used for meditation and focusing her will. At the Boston conference, women were advised to use mirrors on their altars to represent the Goddess. That way, they would be continually reminded that they were the Goddess and that they had divine beauty, power and dignity.

For me, the high point of the conference was the lecture on the Goddess given by Zsuzsanna Budapest, high priestess of the Susan B. Anthony Coven Number 1. Z chose to name her coven after Anthony because of an anecdote she had found in the footnotes of feminist history. When asked if she planned to go to heaven or hell after she died, Susan B. Anthony declared that she intended to go to neither place. When she died she promised to stay right here on earth until the women's movement succeeded. Z was enchanted with this story and promptly invoked Anthony with the name of her coven. (The recent U.S. Department of the Treasury decision to put Susan B. Anthony's likeness on American coins will put Z's coven symbol in the pockets of every American. Anthony's spirit has indeed stayed close at hand!)

At the Boston conference, Z spoke on "The Politics of Spirituality and History of Goddess Worship." She structured her lecture around slides of ancient goddesses and their symbols. Slides of *Yoni* shrines, sacred places carved with images of vaginas, were frequently projected on the screen. "The vagina was worshiped as the source of life," she said. "Sexual energy and life energy are the same. How I wish we had temples like this today!"

Many of Z's slides were of goddesses from ancient Greek culture. I had seen most of the pictures in my college classes on art history and archaeology. In those classes, I had learned the dates, the provenance and the stylistic features of the pieces. In Z's lecture, I learned entirely different things.

Z immediately impressed me as a visionary; perhaps the word prophet is not too strong a term. In her lecture she was speaking of witchcraft in its modern form — of the ways in which contemporary women could free themselves from internalized male values and learn to cherish their own bodies, thoughts and wishes. She saw this as an exciting, wonderful moment in history — as a time when women would leave the religions that taught them to hate their sexuality and led them to distrust their ability to think, plan and will. Her goddess religion, she said, was a good way for women to use their imaginations to create the internal resources needed to feel free and strong. She suggested that images of powerful, wise or athletic women were useful things for a woman to carry around in her mind to help rally psychological energy. Z used her slides of the goddesses of antiquity to provide the women in her audience with visions of female power and beauty. "Just look at the legs of this woman," she exclaimed, pointing to the well-developed calf muscles of a statue known in most art books as the *Dying Amazon.* "This was a culture where weakness was not rewarded," she stated definitively. The Amazon was surely not "dying," Z told us. "At most she was a tad bored."

No scholar of ancient history would want to declare positively that an Amazon culture had ever existed. Most trained academics will discuss the Amazon mythology and make no claims whatsoever about historical fact. Z, however, is free from such scholarly inhibitions. Whenever she lectures, she speaks of myth and history as if they were identical — and for her purposes, they are. Whether mythical or historical, she sees the vision of Amazon culture as the concern of women today. Z's slides of Amazons are meant to provide modern feminists with images of the strong, proud female personalities she wants all women to become. She is consciously using history and myth to inspire women to become twentieth-century Amazons — to have pride in their lives and their ambitions. A year after her Boston lecture, I told Z that scholars of history and classical civilization would be troubled by the use she was making of sculpture and painting. "It doesn't matter," she said with a smile. "Scholars are not the ones who create religions anyway." I had to agree. At that first conference in Boston, Z and other witches like her were functioning as prophets, not as scholars. They were beginning a large-scale religious movement whose goal is to strengthen the mind and will of every woman in Western civilization.

THEALOGY — THE LOGIC
OF GODDESS RELIGION

The teachings or doctrines of modern withcraft should not be referred to as theology. In Greek, *theos* is the word for a masculine god. *Thea* is the word for "goddess" and is a more appropriate root for a term referring to theories of feminist witchcraft. The word *theology* has also come to be used almost exclusively in regard to Christian god-talk. The advent of witchcraft, with its colorful goddess-talk, requires a new term. I hope witches and scholars of feminist religion will adopt my suggestion and name themselves the*a*logians.

Currently, most modern witches use the Old English word *wicca* to refer to a witch as a "wise woman." Etymologists quibble over this usage. About the only fact on which scholars and witches agree is that the first syllable, *wic,* has something to do with words that meant "to bend or twist." The word *wicker* and the Old English term for weave seem to be derived from *wic.* Since modern witches are very concerned with weaving in a metaphoric sense — with weaving spells and learning how to bend the world to their will, I see nothing inappropriate in referring to a witch as "wicca." We can consider the Old English term as having been reborn, so that it actually does mean "wise woman" in current usage.

The image of a woman weaving is a good one to keep in mind when viewing any theory or practice in witchcraft. A woman who weaves is concentrating on changing natural materials into something useful for civilized life. She is skilled at a craft, which she has studied to the point of its becoming second nature. When she weaves she uses this skill to bring something she alone can visualize psychically — like the shape of a basket or the design in a tapestry — into a material form which everyone else can see and use in their world. All witchcraft begins with a psychic picture that a woman works to weave into reality.

In witchcraft, the first thing a woman learns to visualize and bring to birth in the world is herself. She needs to have a positive image of herself at all stages of her life in order to be an effective presence at every age. Likewise, she must be able to conceive of her own growing, changing and aging in ways that do not depress her, but instead foster acceptance and pride.

Many feminists have pointed out how difficult it is for most women in modern culture to accept themselves as they are in any point of their lives. The young girl is constantly directed to tailor her appearance and her personality to catch a man. The married woman is advised to work at staying young to keep her husband's interest, while the older woman is supposed to simply withdraw from life as beauty fades and she can no longer bear children.

Witches use their goddess concept to give women positive self-images in all stages of life. They teach that the feminine life force, i.e., the Goddess, appears in three forms — the maiden, the mother and the crone.

The maiden Goddess is a woman who remains a virgin. Although she may be quite active sexually, the woman is virgin in the sense of being independent of her lovers and free to move and have adventures. All young, unattached women are virgins in this sense as are all women who remain alone for long periods of their lives. The Goddess as virgin is known by many names. Athena, Diana and Kore are three of the most popular.

The mother Goddess is a more nurturing presence. As the adult woman, she is the mother of all life forms. Raising children is considered only one creative possibility for the mother. She could choose to give birth to books, music or a successful business as well. Whenever a woman nurtures either a person or an enterprise, witches consider her a mother. She is acting like the Goddesses known as Demeter, Gaia or Hera in classical mythology.

As the crone, the woman represents the Goddess of wisdom and prophecy. Older women, past menopause, fit the image of the crone — but so do all women who feel old and heavy with life experiences. The crones of the witch community contribute invaluable insight and the perspective of age. Hecate is the most familiar name for this personality of the Goddess.

Witchcraft is the only Western religion that recognizes woman as a divinity in her own right. Mary, the only remnant of a Goddess left in the Christian tradition, is recognized solely because of her son. In contrast, the maiden, mother and crone Goddesses of witchcraft are valued on their own terms. They are honored as independent beings with their own divine styles of experiencing life. The triple Goddess provides imagery of depth and mythic impact, which is completely unavailable to women in any other Western religious tradition.

In addition to elevating the image of woman in religious symbology, witchcraft also improves the idea of woman in secular culture. Because each witch is taught to see herself as the Goddess in all activities, she makes no separation between her religious ideals and her worldly behavior. The triple Goddess allows the witch to envision herself as a regal, valuable being even when she feels unattractive or old — even when she is unattached to any man or to any child. Social pressure to remain forever young and sexy is counteracted, and a woman does not have to justify herself exclusively by the ways she complements the lives of others. Because witchcraft honors several styles of life in its imagery, witches can honor several styles of life in themselves. The Craft encourages a psychological range and flexibility which few other modern philosophies or techniques of self-development can provide for their female adherents.

Acceptance of psychological change is also fostered by linking the triple Goddess to the cycles of the moon. The waxing moon is the maiden, the full moon is the mother and the waning moon represents the crone. Since the cycles of the moon are thought of as related to all human activities, they serve to remind witches of the ebb and flow of all energy for projects and enterprise. Human effort is seen in a realistic fashion. Times of depression and withdrawal are expected and there is no intense pressure to effect major changes in one's life or circumstances immediately. The philosophy of witchcraft is a patient one that encourages steady, gradual transformation.

This attitude toward change guides the procedures for all rituals and spells directed toward self-transformation. At holiday gatherings, for example, Starhawk uses a cup of wine to encourage meditation about gradual change. She passes the cup around the circle and asks each covener to gaze into the wine and envision herself changed in some desirable fashion — either in outlook or in material circumstances. Each witch then swallows just a small sip of the changed picture she has projected into the wine. No sudden alteration is expected. Nevertheless, by visualizing the change, a goal for self-development has been set. By symbolically internalizing that goal in the small swallow of wine, witches hope to initiate a cycle of progress toward it.

With the moon as their main metaphor for growth and development, witches have a theme of a slow and steady process in any work of psychological transformation they might undertake. A place for the waning moon encourages acceptance of inevitable setbacks and regressions as well.

TAROT CARDS

To witches, magic is the ability to bring about change in the world. Each change, they believe, begins with encouraging a favorable psychological attitude toward it. Because they think that an idea must live in the mind before it can live in the world, witches set great store by imaginal life. Most witch magic is concerned with stimulating and focusing the imagination. Props like crystal balls, magic mirrors, incense, candles and interesting jewelry are objects used to capture attention and appeal to playful layers of the mind. Once a witch learns to watch her fantasies and daydreams dance in her mind, she can learn to impose some gentle discipline on the dancers. She gradually develops skill at psychic choreography and can pattern much of her imaginal life as she pleases. When a woman directs her own thoughts, witches believe she starts to direct her own life.

Anyone who would like to witness the skill witches have in rousing the imagination ought to have her or his Tarot cards read. Tarot is a form of spell-casting that uses cards to change the psychological consciousness of two people — the woman reading the cards and the one whose cards are being read. While going through the ritual steps of shuffling and cutting the cards, laying them on a special cloth and lighting a candle or a fragrant stick of incense, the reader gradually focuses her intuitive faculties on the person whose reading she is about to do. While watching these actions, the other person begins to concentrate on the drama about to unfold as the reader turns over each new Tarot image.

Tarot decks consist of seventy-eight brightly painted

cards called *arcana,* the Latin word for "secrets." Each card depicts a moment of life — an event, a mood or a behavior pattern. Because Tarot cards are explicit in their portraits of matters relating to love, death, joy and work, they immediately affect the ideas and emotions of anyone who concentrates on them. In my classes on myth and symbol, I use Tarot cards to teach students how to work with images. I project the Tarot's major trumps on a movie screen and ask the class to describe what they see. My students soon learn that they can understand images — that they know what general feelings, thoughts and actions go along with visual pictures.

Most skilled Tarot readers will discuss the images on the cards with the people whose readings they are doing. People are thus encouraged to think about their lives in relation to the images depicted on the cards. In psychological terms, people are encouraged to project their thoughts and feelings on to the cards in order to examine those projections. In this way, Tarot cards can teach a great deal about the psychological reality one is living in at the time of the reading. Thorough knowledge of the present is essential for any knowledge of the future. By providing us with deeper insights into the present, the Tarot can indeed reveal possibilities for the future.

Tarot readings can be occasions for valuable personal interaction. Some women read each other's cards every week and thus learn a great deal about one another's hopes, fears and aspirations. They become invaluable counselors for each other. A few feminist covens do readings in a group so that several women can contribute insights to each reading. Family readings are possible too. A friend of mine reads cards with her nine-year-old daughter and seven-year-old son. She asks the children to select cards that describe how they feel. The family then discusses the pictures together. Her children love the game and she feels that the cards have helped to bring her family closer together.

A BALANCED WILL

In witchcraft, a woman's will is sacred. Once she has learned to visualize her wishes, a witch uses her will to bring them to reality. Among witches a woman with a strong will is admired and considered an asset in the coven's work. The negative image society has of the headstrong, willful, determined woman is completely reversed in witchcraft. Witches find most of the world's "bitchy," "pushy" females endearing.

The only rule that restricts the play of the will is an injunction not to use it for destructive purposes. The golden rule of the Craft is "Do what thou wilt, so long as it harms none." The reasoning behind this law is based less on a charitable ideal than it is on a sense of balance. Witches believe that everything they do has effects which return to them three times as strong as their initial action. Hexing is dangerous because a witch becomes involved with destructive thoughts that can rebound in her own life. If someone else has wronged a witch, however, she is perfectly safe in avenging herself to whatever degree she suffered harm.

This sense of balance is apparent whenever witches commit acts of even minor violence. A witch who cuts a living branch from a tree to use as a wand, for example, will pay with a drop of her own blood. Perhaps this sense of dialogue with physical matter and with psychic energy is based on the Craft's origins as a nature religion concerned with the growth and harvest of food. On a practical level, the death of plants and animals contributes to new growth. People who are in tune with natural rhythms will of course create religions that correspond to such experiences.

Witchcraft's roots in nature religion and its attention to the cycles of the moon enable it to teach a philosophy that respects life and change. Its triple Goddess concept allows women to adopt this philosophy in ways that enhance their self-respect.

But what about the men? Is there any place for men in feminist witchcraft?

MEN AND THE DYING GOD

Because all forms of witchcraft give the Goddess a male consort known as the Horned God, all forms of witchcraft have the potential for including men in the mythology and rituals of the coven. Just as female witches are considered Goddesses, so male witches are considered Gods. However, in feminist witchcraft, the Goddess is valued more highly than the God, with the result that women have a higher position in the power structure. Some covens reason that since women give birth to men, they have the potential of identifying with the male principle — of seeing men as part of themselves. On the other hand, since men do not give birth to women, they are less likely to identify with female forces. With this understanding, a coven without men can still experience male and female forces. A coven without women, however, cannot function properly.

In a form of feminist Craft called the *Dianic,* men are excluded entirely. Like the ancient goddess Diana, the witches who take her name prefer to hold rituals only in the company of other women. Z Budapest, a Dianic high priestess, believes men should be encouraged to follow traditions other than the Craft. Men, she feels, can serve as helpful sons of women and, perhaps, as lovers, but they should not be considered as equal to women in divinity.

Feminist witches from traditions other than the orthodox Dianic allow men to be initiated as witches and to participate in rituals. Most feminist covens, however, rely on the leadership of women and afford greater prominence to the triple Goddess than to the Horned God. One male witch told me this arrangement seemed fine to him. "Men need to be humble in this time of history," he said. Any man working in a feminist coven needs to share this attitude.

In witchcraft, the Horned God's duty is to make love to the Goddess and delight her. Witches often picture him as Pan, the half-man, half-animal nature god of Greek mythology. He is very dear to the Goddess but is never meant to rule her as a husband or master. He is sexual energy personified — the one who, as Z Budapest says, "makes one-night stands delightful." Many witches feel that women should relate to men in life the way the Goddess relates to Pan in myth. She enjoys temporary alliances with him but neither expects nor needs him for long-term sustenance.

The Horned God's association with the Goddess for short-term periods only is reflected in his life cycle each year. (Witches measure annual time by the moon. Thirteen twenty-eight-day months, or thirteen complete cycles of the moon add up to 364 days of the year. An extra day is added for the birthday of the sun. Since they have no need for making allowances for partial days to compose a leap year, witches feel their method is much more efficient than marking a year the solar way.) The God is born and dies in the space of one thirteen-month lunar year.

On the longest night of the year, the Winter Solstice, witches celebrate the God's birthday as the Sun. They know that the time when sunlight is dimmest and days are shortest is also the time when sunlight will grow stronger and days will begin to lengthen. Witches say that Christ was originally this Sun child, and that like the Sun child he was destined to sacrifice himself after a short life.

The God's mother is the Goddess herself. As the year waxes into spring, her son becomes her lover and their union makes the whole world bloom with sexual energy. The first of May, May Day, is the time for this celebration — probably the most joyous holiday of the witch's year. The famous Maypole represents the God's erect phallus and is used as the rallying point for dancing and playing games.

On the longest day of the year, the Summer Solstice, the Sun God dies in the Goddess's embrace. The time of greatest light is also the time when that light starts to diminish. The grief that the Goddess feels at the death of her consort and son is tempered by the knowledge that she has the power to give him rebirth once again in winter. Like Christ, the Horned God dies only to be born again. Nevertheless, he dies each year and is thus continually involved with the process of dying. His connection to life is solely as the lover of the Goddess.

Christianity, witches say, broke the Sun God's tie with the Goddess. Witches feel that tales of Christ's antiseptic birth together with Christian refusal to see *anything* female as divine amounts to a denial of life. When Jesus Christ set himself apart from women and sexuality, he lost his connection with material joys and earthly dynamics. Christianity, witches say, had to become a religion focused on death, martyrdom and self-denial. Life in this world had to be devalued in favor of some vague notion of life after death.

Witches are deeply concerned with the fate of a culture they see as worshiping a god of death. Such a culture, they feel, is doomed to debase both women and nature because it has lost touch with the divine life force present in women and all natural life. Witches see themselves as harbingers of a vast cultural movement to bring human culture back to life — to bring the wayward Horned God back to his mother and lover. Religion, they feel, should not strive for greater and greater transcendence of this world — for this is a striving toward death. Instead, witches say, religion should return to earth — return to greater involvement in this life and its material, tangible cycles of growth and decay. In order for this to happen, all deities — all goddesses and gods — have to be understood as forces within nature and human beings, within the stuff of life. A male figure who pretends to transcend women, sex and earthly delights cannot bring life into the world — he can only represent death.

Witches are not the only ones who posit a relation between the Judaeo-Christian tradition and disrespect for nature. A number of religious thinkers have suggested that the ecology crisis has been engendered by the derogatory attitude Judaism and Christianity have toward non-human life.[2] They call into question the usefulness of Judaeo-Christian teachings about man's superiority over nature, about *his* destiny to conquer nature and to harness *her* for *his* use. Is it possible, theologians are asking, that these very teachings have spurred man to destroy so much of the world of plants and animals? It certainly is difficult to imagine pagans, with their awe and respect for natural life, killing off whole species or dumping industrial wastes into lakes and rivers. Such actions can be done only by people who think themselves above the material world which spawned them.

If we combine these recent theological investigations into the ecology crisis with the witches' charge that a lone male god must be a death god, we are faced with a serious question. Does the complicity of Judaism and Christianity in the fouling of the environment go deeper than the verbal doctrine of the superiority of man over nature? Could the abuse of the environment be a behavior pattern encouraged by the image of God Himself? Could it be that the image of Christ as God above this life and this world sanctions civilization's disdain for the natural, living world?

Recent psychoanalytic theory suggests that the image of an antiseptic male god cast in the role of savior could very well be a symptom of the direction toward death which human culture seems to have taken. In her brilliant work, *The Mermaid and the Minotaur*,[3] Dorothy Dinnerstein has stated that our view of men as the ones who save us from human suffering and pain is conditioned by our early childcare arrangements. Because women are the ones who bring us into the human condition, who first care for our physical selves when we are babies, it is also women who first fail us in our hopes for never-ending physical satisfaction. We thus come to hold women responsible for the "facts of life" — that is, for bodily sickness, unpleasantness and, ultimately, for death.

Because men have minimal contact with our infant selves, Dinnerstein suggests that they always seem to represent cleanliness, antiseptic order and even immortality. Woman becomes raw nature who must be carefully regulated by man. According to Dinnerstein, we want man to control woman and nature so that our infant experience of being vulnerable to the bodily suffering identified with women will not be repeated. We thus tend to place men in exclusive command of our adult public lives — of our laws, our government and our military activities — with the hope that they will save us from our own mortality. Women, on the other hand, are relegated to the private sphere of culture, where what we feel to be their overwhelming power to harm can be contained. If civilization would involve men in infant care to the same extent as women, Dinnerstein believes that we could no longer identify ills of the flesh exclusively with females. Only then could we involve both sexes equally in the business of running the world.

Dinnerstein sees our present segregation of the sexes and separation of the values each represents as extremely dangerous. By cutting men off from responsibility for our bodily disappointments, we also cut them off from responsibility for basic processes of life. Their activities in the public sphere of culture tend to become distant from life and thus to show disdain for living mortal things. Male public culture gets caught up with machines and puts emphasis on things that are not alive. The decision-making of males in power tends to happen in a vacuum with little reference to the needs of life. Paradoxically, the public leaders who are supposed to help us deny death become increasingly oblivious to life and show increasing contempt for it. We have a civilization in which males in high places imitate a male god in heaven — both think themselves above the petty concerns of simple nurture and delight in generative life.

Because men are raised to feel themselves removed from the needs of human babies, they are often insensitive to the seriousness of initiating enterprises which make the planet toxic and create machines to exterminate life altogether. Dinnerstein feels that both men and women are guilty of allowing our public culture to continue in this anti-life direction. She states that women who accept the myth of being eternally feminine, and who thus remove themselves from the masculine business of running the world, are responsible for isolating life values in the home. If we do not combine the concerns of female private culture with those of male public culture, Dinnerstein sees the prognosis for our civilization as grim.

It is of prime importance to realize that Dinnerstein does not see the roles of the sexes as determined by biology. She does not see women as innately more concerned with the body than are men. She thinks sexual role differentiation to be a direct result of our practice of putting women in exclusive control of human infants. If we were to change this, to involve men in the care of babies from the time of their birth, we would change our perception of what the nature of each sex truly is. Men could become more occupied with bodily life and with cycles of growth and decay and thus could incorporate the values of nurture into their worldly affairs. They could no longer be imagined as beings above it all. Women, on the other hand, would not exclusively represent body and physical life, but would be seen as equally capable of what we now think of as the higher business of civilization. Dinnerstein feels that much more than sexual liberation is at stake. A change in the way we imagine men and women and thus in the way we parcel out their tasks is crucial for the preservation of our race. We must bring our male governing establishment back to earth and the realistic experience of care for living substance.

Perhaps the emergence of the Goddess is one sign that the cultural movement back to earth has begun. In our present situation, in which women are the ones who nurture us, natural life can probably only be imagined with female symbols. The Goddess of feminist witchcraft, with her love of life, her acceptance of death and her presence within the tangible reality of animals, plants and humans, could be an indication that the human race is beginning to grow up. She could signify that more of us are achieving enough psychological maturity to accept mortality and yet to keep our sense of wonder and affirm that life is good. In any case, she is surely a sign that Western religious life is beginning to change. For witches, God has moved from an image of a celibate male above and beyond humanity to an image of a vibrant female who is a part of our physical and psychic life.

This movement should not be trivialized as a mere sex change for God. Modern witchcraft represents a profound shift in the human tendency to imagine gods, goddesses and divine beings as forces outside human selves and to conceive of these beings as interior experiences. The psychological importance of witchcraft cannot be overlooked whatever one may think about pagans, witches or feminists.

WHY WITCHES SCARE SCHOLARS

In her book *New Woman/New Earth,* Rosemary Ruether states that "any effort to achieve a just view of the phenomenon of witchcraft . . . must clear away many layers of tendentious ideology."[4] I think Ruether is basically correct. "Tendentious ideology" — i.e., deep prejudice — handicaps nearly every scholar who has worked on the subject of witchcraft. Even if a researcher is relatively objective, she or he must wade through the work of people with heavy biases — usually against witches and their craft, but sometimes of a more subtle variety.

Often bias takes the form of an effort to rationalize too quickly, to codify the phenomenon of witchcraft and standardize it in a facile historical sense. I am thinking now of the work of scholars like Jules Michelet, who explained witchcraft exclusively as a hopeless effort at organization directed toward peasant revolution in the Middle Ages.[5] The work of Norman Cohn can be mentioned in this context too. Cohn displays a pitiful lack of knowledge about pagan practices such as feast days.[6] Such ignorance makes it easy for him to conceive of witchcraft as a phenomenon more or less imagined by those who persecuted witches. Even Jeffrey Russell's careful scholarship seems to veer off in an irrational direction with his belief that witchcraft was an organized anti-Christian heresy and that there were some witches who did eat babies and who did deserve punishment.[7] Russell's dedication of his book also gives me reason to pause. "To my wife and children," he writes, "who are not quite numerous enough to form a coven, thanks for enabling me to witness the activity of demons firsthand."[8] I tend to mistrust the work of a man who thinks of witchcraft as "a socialized channel for the expression of aggressive impulses"[9] and who lives in a world in which he fantasizes his wife and children as a "coven."

Often the tendentious ideology of scholars simply takes the form of minimizing the number of people who may have been killed by being burned as witches. One former colleague of mine will not admit the possibility that more than a few hundred women were killed in all the years of persecution. Likewise, as Carol Christ has pointed out,[10] there are Jungian scholars who prefer to see the execution of women in a purely symbolic sense. Edward Whitmont labels the mass murders for witchcraft as a mutation in the collective psyche "which temporarily terminates the feminine principle." Whitmont sees these murders as a "necessary price to be paid for individualization and individuation."[11]

These are examples of the prejudice with which scholars and theorists have viewed witchcraft. Such prejudices ought to be taken very seriously by those of us who believe that modern witchcraft should be the object of focused research in the discipline of religious studies. We should be aware of some of the psychological and ideological positions of scholars and clergy that modern witchcraft calls into question. Only then can we understand the reluctance of colleagues to discuss witchcraft as a modern religion and can we hope to put their opposition in proper perspective.

As a first step toward dispelling some of the prejudices involved in the study of the Craft, I have condensed the phenomenology of modern witchcraft into twelve factors that make the religion difficult for many Jewish and Christian scholars of Western religious history to treat objectively. These problem areas might be responsible for the deep prejudice, the tendentious ideology, that surrounds the study of witchcraft as a religion. They are also areas that make both the thealogical statements and ritual acts involved in the Craft a fascinating and important field for research and reflection.

1. *Female deities.* Any religion which deifies a female principle is likely to seem primitive if not truly blasphemous and evil to scholars and clergy.

2. *No body and soul dualism.* Witchcraft does not separate the body from the soul and accord one a more lofty destiny than the other. A Western religion that does not denigrate the human body or see it in need of being elevated by the spirit is difficult for many who will take a religion seriously only if it has an ascetic cast.

3. *Viewing nature as sacred.* Many theologians have

pointed out that Judaism and Christianity consider nature as inferior to "man" — as something to be conquered by "him." (I put *man* and *him* in quotes because I am not pretending that the words are generic. Woman is often seen as nature in Judaism and Christianity, as an inferior being in need of taming and cultivation by "man.") Witchcraft's view of other forms of life as equal to the human form is certainly not shared by Judaism and mainstream Christianity, and not easily tolerated by them.

4. *Value of the individual will.* Witchcraft, like some other occult religions, values the will. There is no guilt attached to asserting one's will and to rallying deities to one's aid. Followers of Judaism and Christianity see the assertion of individual will as something to be avoided unless God wills it also. Attempts to rally physical and psychic resources to achieve an individual goal are considered degenerate forms of magical thought which do not have a religious character.

5. *Spiraling notion of time.* Witchcraft is a religion that does not hold a notion of the linear progress of time to some judgment day of euphoria or catastrophe. Time — in its everyday, annual and large-scale varieties — is lived as circular and repetitive.

6. *Cyclic notion of bodily growth and decay.* Along with the idea of the spiraling nature of time, witchcraft accepts a cyclic pattern of life. The body's growth and decay is accepted as inevitable and not depressing — definitely not a consequence of sin.[12] The triple aspect of the Goddess as maiden, mother and crone in different stages of growth and decay emphasizes this.

7. *No original sin.* Witchcraft has no concept of a primal sin committed by our ancestors nor does it have a concept of a covenant against which one can sin.

8. *No division of good and evil.* Conditions, ideas and abilities can simply be applied to purposes which may be considered good, evil or neutral. Such absence of dogma

for dividing the world into moral absolutes is disconcerting to many people brought up in the Judaeo-Christian tradition.

9. *Absence of a sacred text.* The fact that there is no sacred book in witchcraft compounds the problem of relativism. A pluralism of beliefs is encouraged. One symbol can mean several things to several people and even several things to one person. (Of course there are those witches who would dogmatize and standardize beliefs and practices. But I suggest that the basic structure of the Craft, with its small units of worshipers and its lack of a single sacred text, will defy such efforts.) Because the Craft is not a book religion, it is seen as primitive by most scholars. The work of the academic world is mainly with written documents. The written word is the respected word. A religion that exists in the modern world and does not utilize texts is bound to appear uncivilized in the sense of not "of the civic body" or not "of the polis."

10. *No rigid law of discipline.* The absence of a need for law to keep base human instincts in control is unthinkable to most Christians and Jews. The picture of a person in Jewish, Christian and even Freudian lore is of a being seething with amoral passions which need the control of some sort of law to keep them from wreaking their gluttonous, wicked designs on the self and the planet. This is the lion tamer fantasy of human personality. The Craft subscribes to no such fantasy. Both conscious and unconscious elements of the person are considered self-regulating and self-governing. If there is a task for followers to accomplish, recognition of the cycles of life determines how instincts, will and drive will be rallied to the goal. No higher moral law is called upon to keep any lower nature in check.

Witchcraft's rejection of the Judaeo-Christian notion of the need for law to control inner passions negates the claims of these religions that they represent a major advance in human history. The Craft would claim that Jewish and Christian laws and commandments do not at this time contribute to the betterment of life on earth.

11. *Sex.* Sexuality is but one aspect of life which the Craft does not consider to be in need of elaborate restrictions. The desire one feels for another person is numinous in Judaism, Christianity and witchcraft. Judaism and Christianity, however, respond to the power of sex by forbidding it except under circumstances carefully controlled by law and society. In contrast, witchcraft lets sex follow its own laws to a very large degree. Sex, like ambition, is understood as having its own regulatory principle.

12. *Play.* Play is omnipresent in witchcraft. Rituals always have fun and jokes that are encouraged and truly spontaneous. No such attitude is possible in the Jewish and Christian stance toward worship.

All of these factors make it extremely difficult for Jews and Christians to recognize witchcraft as a religion. If the Craft were a far-off exotic religion of the East or of some isolated islands, perhaps it might be viewed more seriously and, even, beneficently. But this is not so. Witchcraft is a modern religion of growing strengths and numbers. There are live, educated priestesses who are incorporating their religion and practicing their rites in the nuclei of Western civilization. Scholars will not be able to treat the phenomenon as an exotic religious aberration of an alien culture. Because of the problem areas I have outlined, I expect the acceptance of witchcraft as a subject for study to be a troubling phase in the evolution of Religious Studies as a discipline — and thus its acceptance by many lay people as legitimate will be additionally hampered, beyond the normal reluctance and fear.

Chapter 8

THE MIRROR AND MYSTICISM

●

iN ORDER to keep our theology supple and responsive to individual differences and changes, we must remember that all theology — all thinking about deities and godly powers — is done by individual people in particular situations. Human beings of different sexes, ages, races and environments have different experiences of spirituality and religious phenomena.

It took me several years of working among male theologians to realize that most of them do not assume this. Most believe that they speak for everyone when they lecture about things like guilt, love, sin and grace. This naiveté allows them to make definitive statements about the true way in which all people should live and think about these matters. Theologians are ignorant of what every anthropologist knows — i.e., that the forms of our thought derive from the forms of our culture.

A few feminist theologians have bravely started to point this out to the theological establishment. Their work remains relatively unknown and unpublished because their white male colleagues (who usually decide what is published) simply cannot understand how thinkers like Tillich, Niebuhr and Barth may often be expressing thoughts that reflect only white, male experience.

Before going any further, I had better define the word *experience*. This word, which most people understand so easily, presents great problems to many male theologians. One professor of mine insisted that I leave the word experience out of any material I wrote for him because he *did not understand what it meant.* Feminist theologians use the term to refer to feelings, thoughts and sensations that accompany any event.[1] When feminist theologians say that they want to derive their thoughts about God from experience, they are simply saying that they are beginning from what they have known, felt and seen in their lives. Apparently, many male theologians do not believe that their thought has any close relation with their lives. This is probably why talk about deriving theology from experience often strikes them as incomprehensible.

The first move to place theology within the specific content of women's lives was made by Valerie Saiving Goldstein in 1960. In a short essay called "The Human Situation: A Feminine Viewpoint,"[2] Goldstein argued that sin for most women is different from sin for most men. While it is true that men can often be described as sinning because of an overbearing will to power or because of arrogant self-assertion, there are few women whose lives give them the opportunities to sin in such a manner. Goldstein suggested that it made more sense to condemn women for the sins of "triviality, distractibility, and diffuseness; lack of an organizing center or focus; dependence on others for one's own self-definition . . . in short, underdevelopment or negation of the self."[3] Because Protestant theology never addresses itself to these sins, it is really only discussing sin for men. Protestant theologians, Goldstein warned, are probably guilty of identifying their own "limited perspective with universal truth."[4]

Judith Plaskow was fascinated with this insight and in 1975 decided to base her Yale doctoral dissertation on exploring Goldstein's theory. Plaskow titled her dissertation *Sex, Sin and Grace: Women's Experience and the*

Theologies of Reinhold Niebuhr and Paul Tillich. After some battling with those professors who did not want the words *women's experience* mentioned in her title, she began work on what was to become the first Yale dissertation on feminist theology. Plaskow spent over a year wrestling with the problem of how to define women's experience in order to examine whether Niebuhr and Tillich could be considered as adequate spokesmen for that experience. She finally settled on using novels by women writers as the basis for her work, though she was aware of the particularities inherent in this approach.

Plaskow readily acknowledged that because cultures vary, women's experience varies too. She wrote, "There is probably no universal 'women's experience,' but only the experiences of women in particular societies and particular social groups."[5] Thus Goldstein's work inspired Plaskow to turn to imaginal, artistic material to explore women's experience more broadly. Because Plaskow knows that her material is limited by the individual writer and that writer's cultural situation, she can not fall into the trap Goldstein identified as confusing a "limited perspective with universal truth."

When the methodology suggested by theologians like Goldstein and Plaskow is understood by male scholars, centuries of pretense will fall away. The claim that there is a universal God who dispenses universal experiences of His presence will be recognized as the primitive notion that it is. Until male scholars comprehend that their theology is derived from their experience, radical feminist theologians will be the only ones with a realistic notion of their subject.

NEW TESTAMENTS FOR THE NEW AGE

Deriving theology from experience will be a radical direction that religious theory will take in the age after the fall of the father. The use of contemporary fiction as a resource for reflection on new gods, images and metaphors for our new psycho-religious consciousness will become more prevalent. So far, the most extensive work on using literature as sacred text has been done by feminist theologian Carol Christ.

About seven years ago, Christ stopped looking to the Bible and the Jewish and Christian traditions for information about the spiritual experiences of women. Although she found a few stories in biblical tradition that were about women, she did not think it likely that any were actually told by women. "Because women's stories have not been told," Christ says, "women's experiences have not shaped the spoken language of cultural myths and sacred stories." Christ uses the example of Mary to illustrate her point: "Luke wrote, 'But Mary kept all these things, pondering them in her heart' (Luke 2:19). *Her* word never became flesh and dwelt among us. Perhaps no one ever asked her what she was thinking. Perhaps she never heard stories which could give her words for her own experience. Perhaps the man who wrote the gospel narrative simply could not imagine what it felt like to be in her position."[6]

Christ believed that all thinking about God — all theology — is done in the form of story. Story is the way we give shape to our experiences, both when we reflect on them ourselves and when we relate them to others. She perceived a profound handicap for women of Jewish and Christian cultures. They have not been permitted to hear their own stories. "Men," she points out, "have actively shaped their experiences of self and world by creating the stories they have told. Their deepest stories orient them to what they perceive as the ultimate powers and realities of the universe. We women have not told our own stories. The dialectic between experiencing and shaping experience by storytelling has not been in our own hands."[7] Christ is not interested in doing an "old-style confessional theology" by retelling Jesus's parables to satisfy women's need for story. To identify with most of biblical tradition we women have to imagine that we are men and this does violence to our own connection with ourselves.

Christ set off on her own spiritual quest. She began a series of studies of contemporary writers like Margaret Atwood, Doris Lessing and Adrienne Rich to see if and how a spiritual quest was present in the lives of their female characters. She was looking for any dominant themes which emerged as the heroines grew to understand themselves, to sense their own power and value in the world. Christ knows that her quest studies refer to women characters of specific class, race and age. She suggests that "in a pluralistic world, we must give up our search for the single definitive perception of the ultimate and turn instead to timely, perspectival and finally limited perceptions which clearly recognize their rooting in stories."[8] She thus does not claim that there is a *universal* spiritual quest for all women, but rather that there is religious meaning in the uniquely female experiences that women have.

Christ has studied women's accounts of transformations that occur and insights that arise around sex, mothering and abortion. She has noticed a strong inclination in female heroines to realize the "inevitability of death in the life process,"[9] to develop a sense of timing about movements of the birth and maturation of life and thought and to experience visions arising from the Zeitgeist of history.[10] To learn what individual women are and what we might become in the decades ahead, Christ urges us to "seek, discover and create the symbols, metaphors and plots of our own experience."[11]

Although Christ's message is primarily addressed to women, her method of deriving religious theory, image and metaphor from literature will eventually speak to men as well. The biblical tradition will fail first for women but eventually for men. When women no longer permit men to be patriarchs, patriarchal literature will begin to have less relevance to them and they too will have to seek new stories — new scriptures.

Whatever we use to mirror our experience — be it dreams, visions or literature — sacred scriptures of the new age will be in continuous flux. One text will be unable to reflect the infinite diversity of experience possible in a culture that permits a variety of styles of life and thought. There will be many texts to read, mull over, discuss and dream about. And we will change those texts often, knowing that our unwillingness to hold on to any single description of spiritual experience is not proof that we are fickle — it is proof that we are alive.

Can we predict anything about the new gods of the new age, except to say that there will be many of them?

When we study the religious thought of those who have already outgrown the father-god — the witches, the radical feminists, the modern psychologists — we see a direction inward. All of these people tend to place their gods within themselves, to focus on spiritual processes whose values they experience internally. Judging from these harbingers of our new religious culture, the psycho-religious age will be a mystical one. It seems highly likely that the West is on the brink of developing a new mysticism — post-Christian, post-Judaic. It will most probably be a type of mysticism which emphasizes the *continual observation of psychic imagery.*

"THE WATCHER"

Carol Christ has noted that as Doris Lessing's character, Martha Quest, develops a sense of self and the power to prophesize, she notices a "watcher" deep within. She realizes a "soft, dark receptive intelligence . . . an observing presence."[12] Martha knows this presence as "that part of me which watches all the time. . . . The only part of me that is real — that's permanent anyway."[13] In the place where the watcher lived within her, "her whole self cleared, lightened, she became alive, light and aware."[14] Christ and Lessing are indicating a figure whom we are likely to meet with great frequency in the new age of mysticism — in our theories, in our literature and in the deep places of our consciousness.

Cultivation of a presence like the watcher certainly seems to be what is happening in the psychological theories of James Hillman, one of the most interesting psycho-religious thinkers writing today. Hillman is the founder of "archetypal psychology" — a post-Jungian analytic theory of crucial importance in this new age. He puts psychology and religion in the same territory, refusing, as he says, to define these fields "against each other so that they may more easily become each other."[15]

Hillman's thought is stunning in its originality and yet, as he says, curiously "old-fashioned."[16] He returns to the original meaning of psychology as the "logos of the soul" — as the study and enrichment of that ancient *religious* entity known as the *soul.* Hillman's concept of the soul is very similar to Lessing's concept of the watcher. Just as Lessing has introduced mysticism into her novels through the watcher, Hillman has introduced mysticism into his psychology through the soul.

Hillman quotes Keats as saying: "Call the world if you please, 'The vale of Soul-making.' Then you will find out the use of the world. . . . I say 'Soul-making' — Soul as distinguished from Intelligence. How then are souls to be made? . . . How but by the medium of a world like this? This point I sincerely wish to consider because I think it a grander system of salvation than the Christian religion."[17] Hillman shares Keats's high opinion of salvation derived from the development of soul. However, Hillman wants soul understood not as a thing — but rather as a perspective. "By soul," he says, "I mean . . . a perspective rather than a substance, a viewpoint toward things rather than a thing itself." Soul, Hillman goes on to say, is a "mode" of perceiving — "that mode which recognizes all realities as primarily symbolic or metaphorical."[18]

Hillman describes this soul perspective as a steady, continuing presence. "It is as if consciousness rests upon a self-sustaining or ongoing presence — that is simply there even when all our subjectivity, ego and consciousness go into eclipse."[19] He experiences soul as Martha Quest experiences her watcher — as an observing seer who seems more permanent and enduring than even the conglomerate of entities which we refer to as ourselves.

For Hillman, the cultivation of soul is the most important goal we can have in life. It supersedes all the objects of our ambitions, our love affairs, our altruism, our therapy. Through animation of our soul we gain "an increasing conviction of having, then of being, an interior reality of deep significance."[20] Hillman puts even the usual therapeutic goal of "coping" as second to that of the deepening of soul. If knowing our own soul helps us cope, so much the better — but soul comes first. In archetypal psychology, the development of soul takes precedence over such things as family, work and relationships, all the mini-nirvanas of other psychological systems. Archetypal psychologists hold the nurture of soul in as much respect as any religious sect has held its spiritual goal in any period of history.

Faith in soul, Hillman says, comes to us through the awareness of images, images which move "through the shapes of persons in reveries, fantasies, reflections, and imaginations."[21] He especially values the thoughts and fears that drag us down and terrify us. In archetypal psychology, it is the dark gods that move us most. Other psychologies whitewash these forces by reducing them to labels like *repressed anger* or by dulling their sting with drugs. The archetypalists, however, value depression very highly. They feel that it is our fears of death, illness and aging which move much of our lives. They despise modern psychology for trivializing Hades and his retinue.

A good portion of the writing of archetypal psychologists concerns itself with the gods and goddesses of ancient Greece. They consider Greek deities to be images of behavior patterns that are very much alive in our Western consciousness. Greek mythology is more valuable for articulating the principles of a polytheistic, pluralistic psychology than is the sour righteousness of biblical monotheism. Furthermore, the Greeks never underestimated the power of their dark deities. All this fascinates the archetypalists. They people their journals with profiles of figures in the Greek pantheon in order to explore the spiritual and psychological perspectives embodied in the specific images.

Hillman himself has turned to closer scrutiny of the imaginal process per se.[22] He shares my feeling that archetypes create problems for Jungian theory.[23] His latest work acknowledges that archetypes do not have to be specific symbols. Hillman suggests that we use the adjective "archetypal" instead of the noun "archetype" to refer to those psychic images which are particularly important.[24] The adjective archetypal would be a word for the process of valuing an image, dream or fantasy. Any image that moves us deeply and spurs us to reflection can thus be an archetypal image. We do not need Jungian dictionaries or esoteric encyclopedias of ancient myth to tell us what *the* archetypes are. This philosophical move of changing archetype to archetypal is a landmark in Jungian theory. It begins to rise above the petty reification-deification of Jungian terms and leads us to see the actual psychological processes and viewpoints to which the terms refer. In fact, many Jungian nouns, such as *unconscious, ego, anima* and *animus,* need to be seen through in a similar fashion.

Although archetypal psychology is making brilliant advances in the field of psychology and religion by freeing us from the constraints of the old Jungian terminology, it suffers from a major constraint itself. Archetypal psychology has a problem in its use of the terms *literal* and *imaginal.* At first glance, there appears to be no problem. Archetypalists use *literal* to refer to the point at which we stop our imaginal process and declare, "Aha, I know exactly [i.e., literally] what this image means!" We might say the image is "the mother" or "the anima" or "the repressed feeling function." As soon as we make a pronouncement about what the image *is,* we are literalizing. Archetypal psychologists want us to keep the process alive by keeping it imaginal — that is, by letting the image take us from one meaning to another and never making it wholly identical with any particular explanation. I have no difficulty with this use of the terms *literal* and *imaginal.*

The problem begins when the archetypalists use *literal* to refer to the material world and to any action taken in the material world. *Imaginal* is then used to refer to the nonmaterial world and to inaction or pure contemplation. This use of the terms separates imaginal images from literal life and recalls the old dichotomy between spirit and matter — a dualism which Hillman says he abhors. If archetypal psychology does not heal this split in its outlook, it could become a hollow game of intellectualizing, removed from significant dealings with human life.

After all, depth psychology began in life, in the real pains and joys of real people. Freud and Jung derived their theories from the flesh and blood of life around them. They each observed myths like that of Oedipus and the Great Mother affecting the very physiology of their patients. They saw myths and images at work in the literal life functions of eating and making love. Freud and

Jung built their theories around material derived from case studies, from the lives of the human beings who saw them in analysis. In contrast, modern archetypal psychologists refrain from writing about their cases. They seem to feel that the concrete ties between theory and life should not be emphasized.

The richest symbolic systems of Western culture have acknowledged the identity of image and matter. The Greeks built solid temples to their gods and goddesses, poured libations and celebrated feast days. The alchemists burned their fingers in the physical operations required by their quest for the philosopher's stone. Archetypalists cannot expect to advance the insights of the Greeks, the alchemists, Sigmund Freud or Carl Jung very far if they neglect the tie of image and world. This tie must not be considered too gross, too indelicate or too philistine if the new psychology of soul is to have influence.

Hillman has even stated that the death referred to in archetypal psychology is not literal death at all — not medical death — but rather a deliteralized death. "The imaginal perspective [vis à vis death]," he says, "assumes priority over the natural organic perspective."[25] "Deliteralizing" death robs it of its sting in Hillman's psychology. However, in fact, it is the very fear of literal, material death that creates those powerful and terrifying pathological images Hillman pleads with us to *value*. It is the fear of a real material and literal death which spurs us to drink deep of life and meaning.

I believe a radical step needs to be taken. Archetypal psychology must stop its misguided attempt to deliteralize everything. Hillman has said that the sin of literalism is that it fails to recognize that "concrete flesh is a magnificent citadel of metaphors."[26] While I do not dispute the importance of this realization, I think it equally necessary that we understand that metaphors are also flesh, that they are continuous with our bodily selves.

It is true that we must learn to see the "imaginal aspects" of tangible things, as archetypal psychologist Mary M. Watkins has urged.[27] *However, our spiritual depth and progress in the years ahead depend on our ability to see the tangible aspects of imaginal things.*

The intimate tie between image and life is something which feminist theorists can teach psychologists of religion. Women who have analyzed patriarchy know that the image of a white, male God undergirds the whole economic and social system. The picture of a white man in the sky influences the position of every person under that sky. Images of God dictate who will feel worthy in society and who will feel inferior, who will be respected and who will be despised, who will get easy access to the literal, material goods of culture and who will have to fight for those same goods.

Witches know that their physical lives are changed by their images of the Goddess. A woman's feelings about her body undergo joyous transformation if she imagines herself to be in some sense divine. Those who cast spells and work hexes know that thought has effects in the world — that thought *certainly* influences the one who casts the spells and works the hexes and that thought *seems* to operate on other things as well. Ancient and modern occult theory sees matter and spirit on a spectrum of density in which the only difference between the two is the amount of substance moving in each. Perhaps our new psycho-religious philosophies will one day appropriate and expand on the intuitions of witches and occultists about the tie of image to world.

The new mysticism of the West will largely be defined by women and men who will have an increasing awareness of their own physical presence within the philosophies they create. These women and men will not want to deny the value of their literal, bodily selves. Their theories will affirm materiality and will acknowledge that images are flesh as well. It is difficult to say more about the mysticism we will know in the new age of new gods. Only one thing seems certain — it will be a mysticism with guts!

Chapter 9

EXCURSIONS INTO DREAM
AND FANTASY

mEDITATION
on dreams is gaining increasing popularity in modern religious culture. However, there is nothing particularly modern about considering dreams as religious entities. Among the cultures of the ancient world, dreams were highly esteemed as communications from the gods. Dream interpreters were often employed by rulers to help in government by revealing the will of the gods. Many generals took along interpreters on campaigns to help formulate battle plans pleasing to the divinities. In Greece, the god Aesculapius was believed to effect cures through dream visions. He sent the healing visions to suffering pilgrims who slept in his temples after going through prescribed rituals.[1] Vestiges of this ancient dream culture survive in the Old Testament in stories such as that of Daniel interpreting the dream of Nebuchadnezzar.

There are hardly any references to dreams in the New Testament. The belief that Jesus was the only possible revelation discouraged paying attention to the dreams of humanity at large. Even today, churches remain largely suspicious of techniques purporting to give each person direct access to divine knowledge. The institutions have a monopoly on revelation. When individuals claim to experience revelation outside of hierarchical formulae, the churches behave much like big businesses do when they fear that patent rights are being violated. The idea that each person can reach her or his own understanding of divine forces without going through the Church, the Bible or Jesus is revolutionary. Clergymen often label activities involving personal revelation through dreams or visions as "the work of the Devil."

Dream culture thrives in a polytheistic intellectual milieu. By a polytheistic milieu, I mean one which recognizes that there are a variety of forces at work in human life and thought. One can be polytheistic without believing in gods per se. A person may be polytheistic in her or his political, social and aesthetic attitudes simply by recognizing that several dynamics and sets of standards determine people's organization of their world.[2] Monotheists are those among us who always want to "get it all together" — to decide on one overriding principle which will explain all life, all thought and all feeling. Monotheism becomes increasingly untenable as we recognize the rights of people to live out a variety of life styles under a variety of rules.

Sensitivity to dreams requires appreciation of *psychological polytheism.* In dreams, we see a kaleidoscope of moods and images. Some dream pictures are clear, others are vague. Some are pleasant to think of, others are quite distasteful. *Yet all images are parts of ourselves.* By the very fact that we give birth to them out of the physiological, psychological and philosophical stuff of ourselves, dreams are our creations, our children. We feel that they originate in areas of ourselves that we are not usually aware of in waking life. Thus the dream seems to be both "myself" and "itself" — an entity that is experienced as intimate and foreign all at once.

The religious experience to which people who follow their dreams have access is primarily mystical. Reflecting on a dream when awake can put a person into "the middle place" — a psychological locale mentioned in the writings of both mystics and magicians. One has a sense of existing between what is felt as "I" and what is felt as "Not I." People report that when they contemplate dream images they have a sense of progressively seeing through layer after layer of awareness. Metaphors referring to depths abound. "I feel like I am looking into a huge crystal ball and that I can see forever," one of my friends reported. A student who practiced study of his dreams told me he had the sensation of swimming underwater and parting the curtains of seaweed as he moved. I have had similar sensations of downward progression through great depths when I work with my dreams.

The feeling of depth is partially explained by the way we experience memory in dreams. Even a modest effort at the collection of dreams over a period of months can convince us that nothing is ever lost. Detailed pictures of childhood rooms and adolescent schoolmates will pop up in the construction of dreams. Often past moods are presented minus the literalism of past surroundings. We see that all the moments of our lives enjoy an immortality within us. This sense of connection to the past is felt metaphorically as a pull backward and downward. It can give a person a sense of rootedness.

In addition to providing experiences of meditation, following one's dreams deepens the understanding of particular aspects of personality and character. We get to know the psychic constants that operate within us and become better able to accept the contradictions of our strengths and weaknesses. Dream analysis is a gentle form of spiritual discipline that trains us to develop greater psychic agility and range.

Dreams give us glimpses into the mythic dimension of our lives. They let us see the forces that are eternal in our particular selves, forces eternally at work in our past, present and future psychic constitutions. I often describe such knowledge as the understanding of the psychic furniture of our minds and feelings: knowing which chairs to stand on to reach high places, knowing which pipes are prone to leak or even burst and knowing which beds are most comfortable to rest in.

To illustrate what I hope has been a not-too-lyrical description of the religious function of dreams, I will present three of my own dreams as data. I have chosen to use my own dreams because I can vouch for their religious impact on me. I worked on the first two dreams alone and then in classes on dream analysis I have taken or taught in the past few years. The third dream, "The Australian Pioneer," was explored with a group of friends who meet for the specific purpose of investigating the spiritual value of dreams. I hope these examples will both help nondreamers[3] understand what I am talking about and encourage dreamers to explore their dreams from a religious perspective.

THE TURTLE-WATCHERS

This is the text of a dream I had about five years ago:

There is a little man whose job it is to watch the sea. He stands on the shore of a rocky, sunny beach and watches the water with great interest and enthusiasm. Directly in front of him, the water is quite shallow. A plateau, covered with a carpet of green seaweed rises from the sea bottom and creatures of many kinds crawl up from the depths. There is a large green sea turtle who plods along the surface of the plateau. There is also a magnificent red lobster fighting with a large blue barracuda near the edge of the plateau.

The little man is very excited by these things. He jumps about like a delighted child and points at the wonders he is privileged to see. He loves his work.

A blonde woman with bleached hair stands next to him. She too sees the sea creatures but can not share the man's delight. She wants to know what they mean and how to understand them. She has contempt for the little man's simple reactions and rebukes him for being stupid and naive.

This dream is, in general, very satisfying for me to think about. I love watching the sea through the little man's eyes. The mystery and beauty of the slow-moving turtle and the fierceness of the battle between the lobster and the barracuda excite my sense of wonder, and I feel like a child being treated to a circus. The world is sunny and full of things to enjoy when I allow myself to become the character of the little man. He is what I would call a child of nature, someone whose emotions are direct and uncomplicated. He is filled with simple good will toward the world.

The blonde woman is a very different person. When I see the sea creatures through her eyes, I am not at all comfortable. She is a critic who can never just accept the world as it is. It is not enough for her simply to appreciate the things and people around her. She is disturbed by things that do not make sense and has little respect for the man's plain delight in living and observing. Perhaps her hair color is artificial to show that her mind always wants to change things, to alter them in what might be called unnatural ways. The woman is not a happy person. I can feel her envy for the little man as well as her contempt. She wishes she could be as uncritical and accepting of the world as he is, but the sardonic, restless quality of her thinking will not permit this.

This dream has taught me a great deal both about my attitude toward mystery in life and about my capacity for faith. I am both the little man and the blonde woman, both the childlike believer and the cynic who will always doubt. I see every phenomenon in my world from these two perspectives. The sea creatures also can be understood in two ways — both as parts of me that will emerge from psychic depths throughout life and as parts of the external world that I will come to know. However, whatever the turtle, the lobster and the barracuda come to stand for in my experience, I will always be seeing them from two viewpoints. On the one hand, as the little man I will accept and appreciate them as they are. Yet on the other hand, as the woman I will be critical, wanting things to be more and better than they are, always slightly dissatisfied with what the world has to offer.

Some psychologists who work with dreams would want me to "kill off" the blonde woman. They would suggest that I work on combining her intellectually critical perspective with the innocent joy of the little man. This directive approach to my dream would have me imagine only one figure at the water's edge, someone more balanced and well adjusted than either of the two who are there at present. But my imagination would balk at such an effort and refuse to comply. When I try to combine the characters, I can not see the sea creatures and I lose interest in the dream. The presence of both the little man and the blonde woman are necessary for me to look into the depths. I must be in conflict as both people in order to see the things I find so fascinating.

This conflict will make the simple faith of the little man an impossibility for me. The blonde woman would not tolerate such naiveté for very long. Likewise, the childlike man will prevent me from wholehearted acceptance of the woman's analytic perspective. Finally, I have decided that a look at the sea creatures is worth this contradiction.

The dream of the Turtle-Watchers has led me to forgive myself some failings in a way that traditional religious attempts at solace could not.

THE BATTLE OF THE LIZARDS
AND THE WOMEN

Another dream that gave me valuable insight into the deep conflicts within myself was the following:

There is going to be a battle between giant lizards known as "Trasimenes" and human women. The lizards have the power to bewitch some women and get them on their side. They have a special language, which their women learn. The lizards lure one gorgeous young brunette into the forest to be their leader. I see her being drawn to the lizards, wearing riding breeches and carrying a whip. She will ride one of the largest lizards into battle.

The leader of the women is a philosophy professor I knew at Yale. She is short, dark-haired and efficient. She directs the women with their preparations for battle. I picture her wearing Bermuda shorts and assigning battle stations.

I woke from this dream feeling exhausted and very depressed. "No wonder you're tired," said a friend to whom I confided the dream that morning. "You had dinosaurs tramping around in your mind all night." True enough, I thought, and decided to rest as much as possible that day and think about my dream. (I was a graduate student at the time and could enjoy one of the very few luxuries of that vocation — taking a day to do nothing.)

I started work on the dream by checking out the word *Trasimene.* It was strangely familiar to me although I could not remember where I had read it or what it meant. After looking through various dictionaries, I discovered that Trasimene did not mean anything. However, *Trasimeno* did. Trasimeno was the name of a lake in Italy that had been the site of a major battle in the Second Punic War. It was at Lake Trasimeno that Hannibal and his elephants had massacred the Romans in the second century B.C. I must have read about this battle nine years previous to the dream when I was taking a course on Roman history. I was amazed to discover that my mind had actually stored away such a detail and then pulled it out for use in the dream. I was even more surprised when I looked up the battle in the edition of Livy I had used for the course. The battle of Lake Trasimeno was mentioned in just two brief sentences. I marveled at the amount of information our brains must keep in storage.

Livy had described the Carthaginian victory as occurring after a noble battle in which both sides had been especially valiant. I reasoned that there were two major similarities between my dream battle and its historical counterpart. First, both battles were fought with giant animals. Hannibal's side had used elephants to fight the Romans, while the dream battle had replaced the elephants with lizards. Second, both were battles between opposing sides whom I respected. I had admired the Romans and the Carthaginians in my study of ancient history. Likewise, in the dream, I found it equally difficult to decide which side I wanted to win.

My dream battle is, in fact, a conflict between two ways of life, between two ways of thinking. Rationality is represented by the women led by the philosophy professor, while something we might call intuition is embodied in the Trasimenes. It took me several hours of thinking about the dream to realize that both sides had merit. At first, I took the lizards as mere animals, as beings clearly inferior to women. But I could not understand why I was so attracted to them. On further thought I became aware that they used their own language and knew how to communicate by telepathy as well. By calling the lizards Trasimenes, my psyche was alluding to the Carthaginians, a very civilized people who, although different from the pragmatic Romans, nevertheless had a culture well worth respecting.

The lizards had mystery, beauty (in their brunette leader) and an occult intelligence. As reptiles, they represented a more ancient form of life than did the women. Yet they were huge and could, I felt, be very destructive to civilized life. On the other hand, the side consisting only of women stood for a highly rational form of civilization. Their leader taught philosophy and wore Bermuda shorts — a type of garment I had always thought practical but unattractive. The women represented the Romans in the battle and seemed to embody the same clear-sighted pragmatic attitudes toward the world which characterized Roman life.

I have found no resolution to the conflict depicted in this dream. Whenever I think about it, I can not decide which side I am on. The Trasimenes, with their seductive powers and strange knowledge, attract me just as they attract the brunette woman in my dream. Yet I am afraid of the brute destructiveness of which I feel the lizards capable. In contrast, the analytic women are human and approachable. I feel that a fair, equitable rule of law would prevail if they won the battle. However, something would be lost if they killed off the Trasimenes; some sense of mystery and secret source of power would be gone.

The two sides remain divided in my mind to this day. I do not feel that the battle has been fought, the issue settled. The dream's allusions to the ancient life forms of the giant lizards and the ancient history of the Punic Wars indicate that the conflict is an old one in my psyche, a basic one which is a fact of my psychic life.

All of us suffer from conflicts that occur between two (or more) opposing sides. Christianity has simplified this psychic pattern by telling us stories of the battle between good and evil, or between Christ and the Devil. In all forms of traditional religious dualism, one side is chiefly good while the other is chiefly evil. If we accept such prepackaged mythology, we can miss the subtlety and greater personal relevance of our own struggles as revealed in our own dreams. In the Battle of the Lizards and the Women, neither side is all good or all bad. Both the Trasimenes and the practical-minded women have good and bad qualities. I would lose a great deal if either side destroyed the other. It gives me far more insight into myself and my perceptions to live with an awareness of the nuances and complicated nature of my own conflicts than to try to adhere to a creedal formulation of warfare between good and evil.

Whenever we place the truth of a general doctrine ahead of the truth of our experience, we lose contact with the facts of our own psychic lives. This is the danger in uncritical acceptance of religious or psychological generalities. Note that there are no female anima nor male animus figures in my battle dream, although the conflict is certainly between rational forms of thought and more intuitive perceptions. The categories that religion and psychology give us to explain the world are helpful only in calling attention to features of our lives that we might otherwise miss. But these categories can stifle our thoughts and feelings if we allow ourselves only to value experiences that fit prescribed formulae. Paying close attention to dream figures without attempting to define them prematurely can help us recognize the infinite variety of psychic life, a variety that defies attempts at facile classification.

I hope that my analysis of the Turtle-Watchers and the Battle of the Lizards and the Women will lead some of my readers to see the wealth of spiritual experience that can be revealed in dream life. Before leaving the subject of dreams, I want to describe a recent attempt at exploring dream imagery with a group of women. This experience has convinced me that people can help each other with the highly individualized form of religious development that is fostered by dream awareness. Although a person's dream life may be completely unique in its imagery, it can nevertheless be a focus for communal religious activity.

THE AUSTRALIAN PIONEER

Over the last few months, I have been experimenting with dream analysis in a feminist group. The group uses a technique of dream exploration involving two people, the dreamer and the questioner. The dreamer first describes as much of the dream as she can remember. She then closes her eyes and the questioner asks her more about the dream in order to encourage her to explore further. The questioner may ask the dreamer to walk around the landscape of the dream, to open dream doors or look through dream windows. Sometimes the questioner asks the dreamer to become characters in the dream other than the one she has identified as "I."

All questions are asked for the purpose of helping the dreamer learn more about herself through the dream images. No one is forced to visualize things she prefers to leave unexplored. The group also recognizes that dream images have a certain autonomy and although one may look at an image closely and even change it dramatically, the imagination works by its own rules and cannot be pushed into just any direction. Having one person (or several people) serve as questioners frees the dreamer from having to select avenues of inquiry and allows her to concentrate entirely on the dream picture itself.

I learned a great deal when the group guided me through one particular dream I had had two years ago about Australia. I still had a sense of mystery, excitement and some fear whenever I thought about it. This was the dream text as I related it to the group:

I arrive in Australia, a place I have never seen but which I have wanted to visit for some time. I am told that I must remain in Sydney, which was in the middle of Australia, for five full days before going to any other part of the continent. This news fills me with anxiety. Somehow the thought of being surrounded by so much space for five entire days is very disquieting. I feel it will be one of the most difficult things I have ever done. Staying on the coast would be easier, while being in the interior makes me tremble. I try to be calm and accept the order to stay in Sydney.

The first thing I do is hitch a ride to the grocery store to get provisions. The driver is a friendly man who is glad for my company since the grocery store is over a hundred miles away. We set off on the highway and I look at the landscape as he drives. I feel calmer now that I seem to be coping with the interior, but I am still very excited and quite nervous as the car goes along.

I remembered a mixed sensation of thrill and fear on first awakening from the dream. When I had asked a friend who is a prominent Jungian analyst to help me understand the images, he told me that "the dream shows you are afraid of your own depths." This interpretation seemed true enough. Nevertheless, although I was afraid of the Australian dream space, I was also intrigued by it. I certainly enjoyed thinking about the dream and would periodically borrow books on Australian geography and even went so far as to check out air fares to the continent. All my thoughts and behavior connected with the dream were characterized by a sense of expectancy and excitement about new possibilities mingled with fear of the emptiness in the interior.

When I presented the dream to my group, the questioner tried to coax me to explore the terrain around Sydney. She then asked me to describe my view from the car window in greater detail. I could tell her about the soil and plant life and eventually I could describe a far-off figure who was walking about a mile away from the car. I had never known this person in the original dream. The figure was a man — very tall and suntanned, with a lined and interesting face. I had no trouble describing him in detail even though I was viewing him from a long distance in the dream.

The questioner asked me to become the figure. I could do so easily. When I was able to feel myself to be the man I could watch the car with my dream self and the friendly driver speed past. I had a wonderful sensation of peace as I became him. He was a brave, clear-sighted person who was pioneering alone in Australia. I felt the strength and independence of his character. My fear of the interior vanished along with all other anxieties I was feeling at the moment. I felt calm and at peace with myself and with all of my surroundings. The questioner in my dream group had led me to what I describe as an "experience of grace."

The Australian Pioneer is a psychic figure to whom I have access whenever I feel fearful of the directions that my research, my writing or any other part of my life are taking. For the present, when I imagine the world through the pioneer's eyes I see with a sharp clarity and feel my environment charged with mystical significance.

Further work on the dream in the feminist group has enabled me to see the Australian pioneer as a woman. When I first began to imagine her, she appeared far-off, a blonde woman with a face similar to that of the man. She then approached nearer the car, which I could imagine as stopped. She came much closer than the man ever had. With her standing close to me, I could begin to imagine myself getting out of the car and doing my own pioneering. As I work with the female image, I have a sense of incorporating greater portions of the pioneer's sense of peace and independence into my intellectual and emotional life. I experience this as a religious activity which, for me, is more meaningful than any institutional religious formulation has ever been.

Working with Jung's theory of "dreaming the dream onward" with a group of friends is especially satisfying. Such dream groups actually form a psycho-spiritual community in which the process of symbol formation is shared. For me, the success of my experiments indicates that people probably do not have to enforce a standardized set of religious images on everyone in order to feel a sense of community. Instead, a common ground may be developed around the activity of image-making itself. In this way, the psychic creativity of individuals can be encouraged within the company of a supportive social group. Much more pioneering needs to be done and I look forward to the work that excursions into the psychic interior are bound to produce.

NOTES

CHAPTER 1 — THE END AND THE BEGINNING

1. A *minyan* traditionally refers to the group of ten *men* needed to begin a Jewish worship service. In Orthodox practice a service cannot begin even if 100 women and nine men are present.

2. An example of a Jewish feminist publication is *Lilith: A Quarterly Magazine* (Lilith Publications, Inc., 500 E. 63rd St., Suite 16C, New York, N.Y., 10021).

3. "Excerpts from Vatican's Declaration Affirming Prohibition on Women Priests," *New York Times*, January 28, 1977, p. A8.

4. *New York Times*, January 28, 1977, p. A8.

5. *New York Times*, January 28, 1977, p. A8.

6. See, for example, "Ann Lee: The Messiah as Woman," in *Women and Religion — A Feminist Sourcebook of Christian Thought*, eds. Elizabeth Clark and Herbert Richardson (New York: Harper & Row, 1977), pp. 161-72. See also Susan Setta, "Denial of the Female: Affirmation of the Feminine. The Father-Mother God of Mary Baker Eddy," in *Beyond Androcentrism — New Essays on Women and Religion*, ed. Rita M. Gross (Missoula, Montana: Scholars Press, 1977), pp. 289-301.

CHAPTER 2 — NO FEMINIST CAN SAVE GOD

1. Aileen S. Kraditor, *The Ideas of the Woman Suffrage Movement 1890-1920* (New York: Columbia University Press, 1965; Garden City, New York: Anchor Books, 1971), p. 66.

2. Elizabeth Cady Stanton and the Revising Committee, *The Original Feminist Attack on the Bible: "The Woman's Bible"* (New York: European Publishing Co., 1895; reprint ed. Arno Press, 1974), pt. 1, p. 8.

3. Stanton, pt. 1, p. 110.

4. Stanton, pt. 2, p. 19.

5. Stanton, pt. 1, p. 40.

6. Stanton, pt. 2, p. 8.

7. Elizabeth Cady Stanton, *Eighty Years and More: Reminiscences 1815-1897* (New York: Schocken Books, 1973), p. 452.

8. Alice Stone Blackwell, *Lucy Stone: Pioneer Woman Suffragist* (Boston: 1930), pp. 15-16, 59. Barbara Welter quotes this comment in "Something Remains to Dare — Introduction to '*The Woman's Bible*,'" "*The Woman's Bible*," p. xvi.

9. Rosemary Ruether, ed., *Religion and Sexism — Images of Women in the Jewish and Christian Traditions* (New York: Simon & Schuster, 1974).

10. Ruether, p. 179.

11. Clara Maria Henning, "Canon Law and the Battle of the Sexes," in Ruether, p. 288.

12. Bernard P. Prusak, "Woman: Seductive Siren and Source of Sin?," in Ruether, p. 107.

13. Judith Hauptman, "Images of Women in the Talmud," in Ruether, p. 210.

14. Sheila Rowbotham, *Hidden from History* (New York: Random House, 1974), pp. xx.

15. Ruether, p. 12.

16. Sharon Neufer Emswiler and Thomas Neufer Emswiler, *Women & Worship — A Guide to Non-Sexist Hymns, Prayers and Liturgies* (New York: Harper & Row, 1974).

17. Emswiler, p. 3.

18. Emswiler, pp. 4-6.

19. Emswiler, p. 35.

20. Emswiler, p. 36.

21. Emswiler, p. 36.

22. Letty M. Russell, "Women and Ministry," in *Sexist Religion and Women in the Church — No More Silence!*, ed. Alice L. Hageman (New York: Association Press, 1974), p. 59.

23. Letty M. Russell, "A Feminist Looks at Black Theology," *Women's Caucus — Religious Studies Newsletter* 2:4 (Winter 1974), 4.

24. Letty M. Russell, *Human Liberation in a Feminist Perspective — A Theology* (Philadelphia: The Westminster Press, 1974), p. 51.

25. Russell, *Human Liberation*, p. 52.

26. Russell, *Human Liberation*, p. 103.

27. Russell, *Human Liberation*, pp. 80-81.

28. Peggy Ann Way, "An Authority of Possibility for Women in the Church," in *Women's Liberation and the Church*, ed. Sarah Bentley Doely (New York: Association Press, 1970), p. 77.

29. Way, p. 82.

30. Way, p. 91.

31. Way, p. 94.

32. Rosemary Ruether, *Liberation Theology* (New York: Paulist Press, 1972), p. 48.

33. Sallie TeSelle, *Speaking in Parables: A Study in Metaphor and Theology* (Philadelphia: Fortress Press, 1975), p. 7.

CHAPTER 3 — OEDIPAL PRISONS

1. For an evaluation of Freudian theory as a system describing patriarchy, see Juliet Mitchell, *Psychoanalysis and Feminism* (New York: Random House, 1974; Vintage Books, 1975).

2. Sigmund Freud, *The Standard Edition of the Complete Psychological Works of Sigmund Freud*, 24 vols., ed. James Strachey (London: Hogarth Press, 1953–1974), vol. XXI, p. 27. All quotations are from the edition reprinted in 1973. Hereafter SE will be used to refer to *The Standard Edition*.

3. Freud, SE XXIII, p. 81.

4. Freud, SE XXIII, p. 136.

5. Freud, SE XVIII, p. 135.

6. Freud, SE XXII, p. 162.

7. Eva Figes, *Patriarchal Attitudes* (Greenwich, Conn: Fawcett Publications, 1970), p. 138.

8. Freud, SE XVIII, p. 122.

9. Freud, SE XXI, p. 74.

10. Freud, SE XXI, p. 74.

11. Freud, SE IX, p. 125.

12. Freud, SE XXIII, p. 134.

13. Freud, SE XXIII, p. 135.

14. Freud, SE XXIII, p. 88.

15. Freud, SE XXI, p. 48.

16. Freud, SE XXI, p. 48.

17. Freud, SE XIX, p. 32.

18. Freud, SE XIX, p. 177.

19. Freud, SE XIX, p. 178.

20. Freud, SE XIX, pp. 257–58.

21. See, for example, Kate Millett, *Sexual Politics* (Garden City, N.Y.: Doubleday, 1970), p. 187.

22. Freud, SE XXIII, p. 194.

23. Freud, SE XXI, p. 48.

CHAPTER 4 — WHEN FATHERS DIE WE ALL TURN INWARD

1. Judy Chicago, *Through the Flower, My Struggles as a Woman Artist* (New York: Doubleday, 1977).

2. Chicago, p. 18.

3. C. G. Jung, *Memories, Dreams, Reflections*, ed. Aniela Jaffe,

trans. Richard and Clara Winston (New York: Random House, 1973).

4. Freud, SE IV, p. XXVI.

5. All my thinking about parental roles has been much influenced by conversations with Dorothy Dinnerstein and by her work *The Mermaid and the Minotaur* (New York: Harper & Row, 1976).

6. Freud, SE VI, pp. 258-59.

7. Judith Rossner, *Looking for Mr. Goodbar* (New York: Pocket Books, 1977), pp. 269-70.

8. Freud, SE XXII, pp. 79-80.

9. Freud, SE XXII, p. 80.

10. Freud, SE XXIII, p. 300.

CHAPTER 5 — JUNGIAN PSYCHOLOGY AND RELIGION

1. Ernest Jones, *The Life and Works of Sigmund Freud*, vol. 2 (New York: Basic Books, 1955), pp. 67-68.

2. Sigmund Freud and C. G. Jung, *The Freud/Jung Letters*, ed. William McGuire, trans. Ralph Mannheim and R. F. C. Hull (Princeton, N.J.: Princeton University Press, 1974), p. 295.

3. *The Freud/Jung Letters*, pp. 293-94.

4. *The Freud/Jung Letters*, pp. 293-94.

5. C. G. Jung, *The Collected Works of C. G. Jung*, 20 vols., ed. William McGuire et al., trans. R. F. C. Hull, Bollingen Series XX (Princeton, N.J.: Princeton University Press, 1954-), vol. 11, par. 496. All subsequent references to *The Collected Works* will appear as CW, followed by the volume number and the specific paragraph.

6. Jung, CW 11, par. 496.

7. Jung, CW 10, pars. 159-60.

8. For Jung's version of this story, see Jung, CW 9, pt. 1, par. 233.

9. Otto Rank in CW 18, par. 1284. For more discussion of racism and sexism in Jung's work, see Naomi R. Goldenberg, "A Feminist Critique of Jung," *Signs* 2:2 (Winter 1976), 443-49.

10. Jung, CW 10, par. 95.

11. Jung, CW 10, pars. 96-97.

12. Jung, CW 10, par. 243.

13. Jung, CW 9, pt. 2, par. 29.

14. Jung, CW 9, pt. 2, par. 27.

15. Jolande Jacobi, *The Psychology of C. G. Jung* (New Haven: Yale University Press, 1971), pp. 117-18.

16. Erich Neumann, *The Great Mother: An Analysis of the Archetype*, trans. Ralph Mannheim (Princeton, N.J.: Princeton University Press, 1972), and Esther Harding, *Women's Mysteries* (New York: Bantam Books, 1971).

17. Merlin Stone, *When God was a Woman* (New York: Harcourt Brace Jovanovich, 1977.)

18. See chapter VII, "Feminist Witchcraft: The Goddess Is Alive."

19. Jung, CW 8, pars. 343–442.

20. C. G. Jung, *Memories, Dreams, Reflections*, ed. Aniela Jaffe, trans. Richard and Clara Winston (New York: Random House, 1963), p. 36.

21. Jung, *Memories*, p. 36.

22. Jung, *Memories*, p. 39.

23. Jung, *Memories*, p. 40.

24. Jung, *Memories*, p. 40.

25. Jung has discussed work with patients and "individual revelation" in his correspondence with W. E. Hocking. See C. G. Jung, *Letters I: 1906–1950*, eds. Gerhard Adler and Aniela Jaffe, trans. R. F. C. Hull (Princeton, N.J.: Princeton University Press, 1973), p. 270.

26. Jung, CW 14, par. 749.

27. Jung, CW 3, pars. 388–424.

28. Jung, CW 3, par. 404.

29. Jung, CW 10, pars. 276–332.

30. Jung, CW 10, par. 313.

31. Jung, CW 10, par. 330.

32. C. G. Jung, *Letters II: 1951–1961*, eds. Gerhard Adler and Aniela Jaffa, trans. R. F. C. Hull (Princeton, N.J.: Princeton University Press, 1975), p. 630.

CHAPTER 6 — AND FROM HIS CORPSE THERE FIRST AROSE LILITH, MARY, THE SISTERHOOD AND ANDROGYNES TO TAKE HIS PLACE

1. From the *Alphabet Ben-Sira*. See *Lilith: A Quarterly Magazine*, 1:1 (1976), p. 5.

2. Judith Plaskow Goldenberg, "Epilogue: The Coming of Lilith," in *Religion and Sexism*, ed. Rosemary Ruether (New York: Simon & Schuster, 1974), pp. 341–43.

3. *Lilith*, 1:1, p. 3.

4. Mary Gendler, "The Restoration of Vashti," in *The Jewish Woman*, ed. Elizabeth Koltun (New York: Schocken Books, 1976), pp. 241–47.

5. Marina Warner, *Alone of All Her Sex: The Myth and Cult of the Virgin Mary* (New York: Alfred A. Knopf, 1976).

6. Pat Driscoll, "Daring to Grow," in *Women in a Strange Land*, eds. Clare Benedicts Fischer, Betsy Brenneman, and Anne McGrew Bennett (Philadelphia: Fortress Press, 1975), p. 64.

7. Driscoll, p. 64.

8. Patricia Martin Doyle, "Women and Religion: Psychological and Cultural Implications," in Ruether, p. 39.

9. Wayne A. Meeks, "The Image of the Androgyne: Some Uses of a Symbol in Earliest Christianity," *History of Religion* 13 (February 1974), 165-208.

10. Meeks, p. 207.

11. Meeks, p. 208.

12. Mary Daly, *The Church and the Second Sex*, 2nd ed. (New York: Harper and Row, 1975), p. 22.

13. Carolyn Heilbrun, *Toward a Recognition of Androgyny* (New York: Harper & Row, 1974).

14. Heilbrun, pp. ix-x.

CHAPTER 7 — FEMINIST WITCHCRAFT — THE GODDESS IS ALIVE!

1. Miriam Simos (Starhawk), *The Spiral Dance* (San Francisco: Harper & Row, 1979).

2. See, for example, Lynn White, "The Religious Roots of our Ecological Crisis," *Science*, 155 (1967), 1203-7.

3. Dorothy Dinnerstein, *The Mermaid and the Minotaur* (New York: Harper & Row, 1976).

4. Rosemary Ruether, *New Woman/New Earth* (New York: Seabury Press, 1976), p. 93.

5. Jules Michelet, *La Sorcière* (Paris: P. Viallaneix, 1966).

6. Norman Cohn, *Europe's Inner Demons* (New York: Basic Books, 1975), p. 117. Cohn wrongly considers feast days as holidays initiated in defiance of Christianity and not as sacred days which antedate the Christian religion entirely.

7. Jeffrey Burton Russell, *Witchcraft in the Middle Ages* (Secaucus, N.J.: The Citadel Press, 1972).

8. J. B. Russell, p. viii.

9. J. B. Russell, p. 276.

10. Carol Christ, "Some Comments on Jung, Jungians and the Study of Women," *Anima* 3:2 (Spring 1977), 66.

11. Edward C. Whitmont, "The Momentum of Man," *Anima* 3:2 (Spring 1977), 47.

12. Marina Warner, *Alone of All Her Sex: The Myth and Cult of the Virgin Mary* (New York: Alfred A. Knopf, 1976).

CHAPTER 8 — THE MIRROR AND MYSTICISM

1. For a similar definition, see Carol P. Christ, "The New Feminist Theology: A Review of the Literature," *Religious Studies Review* 3:4 (October 1977), 212 n. 3.

2. Valerie Saiving Goldstein, "The Human Situation: A Feminine Viewpoint," in *The Nature of Man in Theological and Psychological Perspective,* ed. Simon Doniger (New York: Harper & Row, 1962), pp. 151–70.

3. Goldstein, p. 165.

4. Goldstein, p. 151.

5. Judith E. Plaskow, "Sex, Sin and Grace: Women's Experience and the Theologies of Reinhold Niebuhr and Paul Tillich" (Ph.D. diss., Yale University, 1975), p. 47.

6. Carol P. Christ, "Spiritual Quest and Women's Experience," *Anima* 1:2 (Spring 1975), 5.

7. Christ, p. 4.

8. Christ, p. 7.

9. Carol P. Christ, "Margaret Atwood: The Surfacing of Women's Spiritual Quest and Vision," *Signs* 2:2 (Winter 1976), 316–30.

10. Carol P. Christ, "Explorations with Doris Lessing in Quest of *The Four-Gated City,*" in *Women and Religion,* rev. ed., eds. Judith Plaskow and Joan Arnold (Missoula, Montana: American Academy of Religion and Scholars Press, 1974), pp. 31–61.

11. Christ, "Spiritual Quest and Women's Experience," p. 7.

12. Doris Lessing, *The Four-Gated City* (New York: Bantam Books, 1970), pp. 38–39. Quoted and discussed by Carol Christ in "Explorations with Doris Lessing in Quest of *The Four-Gated City.*"

13. Lessing, p. 238; Christ, "Explorations with Doris Lessing in Quest of *The Four-Gated City,*" p. 42.

14. Lessing, p. 238; Christ, "Explorations with Doris Lessing in Quest of *The Four-Gated City,*" p. 42.

15. James Hillman, *Revisioning Psychology* (New York: Harper & Row, 1976), p. 168.

16. Hillman, p. ix.

17. H. B. Forman, ed., *The Letters of John Keats* (London: Reeves & Turner, 1895), letter of April 1819, p. 326. Hillman quotes this passage in *Revisioning Psychology,* p. ix and p. 231 n. 1.

18. Hillman, p. x.

19. Hillman, p. x.

20. Hillman, p. 50.

21. Hillman, p. 50.

22. James Hillman, "An Inquiry into Image," *Spring — An Annual of Archetypal Psychology and Jungian Thought* (Zurich: Spring Publications, 1977), pp. 62–88.

23. Naomi R. Goldenberg, "Archetypal Theory After Jung," *Spring — An Annual of Archetypal Psychology and Jungian Thought* (Zurich: Spring Publications, 1975), pp. 199–220.

24. Hillman, "An Inquiry into Image," p. 84.

25. Hillman, *Revisioning Psychology,* pp. 207–208.

26. Hillman, *Revisioning Psychology,* p. 174.

27. Mary M. Watkins, *Waking Dreams* (New York: Harper & Row, 1976), p. 148.

CHAPTER 9 — EXCURSIONS INTO DREAM AND FANTASY

1. For an excellent description of such ritual procedures in the ancient world, see Mary M. Watkins, *Waking Dreams* (New York: Harper & Row, 1976). For a modern experiment with the efficacy of the technique, see Henry Reed, "Dream Incubation: A Reconstruction of a Ritual in Contemporary Form," *Journal of Humanistic Psychology* 14 (1974).

2. David L. Miller, *The New Polytheism* (New York: Harper & Row, 1974), and James Hillman, "Psychology: Monotheistic or Polytheistic?," *Spring — An Annual of Archetypal Psychology and Jungian Thought* (Zurich: Spring Publications, 1971), pp. 193–208.

3. Sleep research indicates that we all dream. Not all of us, however, remember our dreams. "Non-dream-rememberers" is perhaps a more accurate term than "Non-dreamers."

INDEX

Abraham: 12
Adam: 72-73
Ahasuarus: 73-74
Amazon culture: 95
Androgynes: 78-81
Anima/animus theory: 57-61, 124
Anthony, Susan B.: 10-11, 94
Archetypal psychology: 121-125
Archetypes, concept of: 54-64

Baptism: 79
Bible: Jung on, 66; legalistic
  challenges to, 11-12; on ordination, 21; on position in the
  church, 11; rebels of, 72-74;
  relativism, 3, 10-13; retranslation, 18-21; sexism in, 19-20
Biblical characters: 12
Blacks: African, 55; American, 54
Body and soul dualism: 111
Boston conference on women's
  spirituality: 92-94, 96
Budapest, Zsuzsanna: 94-96, 103-
  104

Castration anxiety: 32-33
Catholic church: Jung on, 49-51;
  myth and mystery, 49; ordina-
  tion of women, 5-6; see also
  Christian religions
Chicago, Judy: 39
Christ, Carol: 110, 118-119, 120-
  121
Christ, Jesus: 22, 23, 63, 105
Christian religions: challenges to,
  8-9; defense of, 21; and ecology,

106, 112; equality in, 6-7; Freud
  on, 26-30; psychology of, 5;
  reformism, 15-16; witches' view
  of, 90
Church property: 12
Church services: 18-19
Classical religion, 23-24
Cohn, Norman: 110
Community: 53-54
Consciousness-raising: 1-2
Coven: 103, 110
Cyclic pattern of life: 112, 113

Daly, Mary: 26, 80
"Daring to Grow" (Driscoll): 76
Death: 105, 106, 125
Deborah: 12
Depression: 123
Dianic: 103
Dinnerstein, Dorothy: 106-109
Disciples, in general: 51-52
Discipline, in feminist witchcraft: 113
Dream culture: 128-129
Dreams: analysis of, 130-140; Jung
  on, 66-68; religious function of,
  67-70
Driscoll, Pat: 76-77

Ecology crisis: 106
Ego: 44, 124
Emswiler, Sharon Neufer: 18-20
Emswiler, Thomas Neufer: 18-20
Equal Rights Amendment (ERA): 91
Eros: 57, 59-60
Eternal validity of Bible: 20
Ethics: 46-47

149